Sept. 28, 2016
ENJOY ! ! !

†† SHANTEL A. OLIVER-LOVALLEN

PrayerWorks

PRAYERWORKS

THE POWER THAT AWAITS BELIEVERS

PAUL EGURIDU

DESTINY IMAGE® PUBLISHERS, INC.

P.O. Box 310, Shippensburg, PA 17257-0310

"Speaking to the Purposes of God for This Generation and for the Generations to Come."

This book and all other Destiny Image, Revival Press, MercyPlace, Fresh Bread, Destiny Image Fiction, and Treasure House books are available at Christian bookstores and distributors worldwide.

For a U.S. bookstore nearest you, call 1-800-722-6774.

For more information on foreign distributors, call 717-532-3040.

Reach us on the Internet: www.destinyimage.com.

Trade Paper ISBN-13: 978-0-7684-3270-1

Hardcover ISBN-13: 978-0-7684-3495-8

Large Print ISBN-13: 978-0-7684-3496-5

Ebook ISBN-13: 978-0-7684-9095-4

For Worldwide Distribution, Printed in the U.S.A.

1 2 3 4 5 6 7 8 9 10 11 / 13 12 11 10

Acknowledgments

First my acknowledgment goes to the many readers of this book and to you. I thank you for taking the time to read and internalize every page. My hope is that you will make prayer a vital part of your life and become "God's power house" on earth.

Next, I want to express my deep indebtedness to each of the following:

My Generals in the School of Prayer: Archbishop Nicholas Duncan William, Late Apostle Joseph Ayodela Babalola, Pastor E.A. Adeboye, Evan Roberts, Late Dr. Bill Bright, Dr. David Yonggi Cho, Late Rev. Andrew Murray, Pat Robertson, Loren Cunningham, Dr. D.K. Olukoyo, Late Archbishop Benson Idahosa. Your prayer investment, along with that of other countless apostles of prayer with the cloud of witnesses, has kept this generation from decadence.

William Hill: This book is about prayer accomplishments; William is one of the proofs of a cry for an open Heaven in my life and ministry. The birth of this book was actually in his home, a safe haven for me. His coming into my life was like a breath of fresh air. Thanks for being a very faithful prayer partner and a dear coventant friend for these many years.

Bishop Bart Pierce: Thanks for challenging me to take a bold step of faith in taking this book to another level. I have learned under your covering that a true mentor is not a friend, but one who provokes you to rediscover who you really are, motivating you to reach your full potential.

Steven Peters: My faithful spiritual son and best friend in ministry, you are one of the reasons God sent me to North America. Thanks for standing with me these many years.

Joseph Sproviero: My dear friend and spiritual son, born in due season, thank you for standing with me during my most difficult times; your investment in my life and ministry still counts.

Murray and Sharon Gersuk: You are the unbeatable couple—my personal assistants, my behind-the-scenes support, my helpers in every possible way to make my goals a delightful reality. I want you to know that all the money in the world could never buy anything that could replace our relationship. I am deeply grateful for your priceless efforts in keeping me and this book in your prayers.

Ken Walker: My introduction to Ken was an answer to prayer during the writing of this book. Really, you are one of the best ghost writers I have ever met. Your work with *PrayerWorks* speaks for itself. Thanks for the excellent job.

Gopal Raju: Thank you for giving me the opportunity to put prayer to work in December 2004 in your home. The outcome was the birth of your second son: "If I be a man of God, let there be a cry of a baby in this house according to the seasons of life." The answer to this prayer has been one of the bedrocks of my confidence in God during critical times.

Kingsley Emelogu: It is good to have people in life who truly believe in me. Kingsley is one of them. I stand in amazement at the extraordinary confidence he has in me. How do I acknowledge someone who still believes in me when all things are against me? There are no words, just love.

Helga Walz: You are my faithful secret warrior, praying for me while in the mission field. Thanks for all your labor night and day in prayer so that I can remain under open heavens.

Pastor Errol and Kim Beckford: My covenant friends, your church was the altar for my sacrifice that still speaks today. Thanks for your unselfish support these many years.

Pastor Pinak and Ratna Maitra: I really do not have words to describe my complete affection for this couple. They are practical examples of what true Christianity is all about. Thanks for making a difference.

Pastor Victor and Judith Emenike: Your steadfast commitment to take the message of healing and miracles to nations of the world will not go unrewarded. Thanks for being my treasured friends.

Bishop Edem Hopeson: Thank you for giving me the opportunity to prove my calling under your covering while I was a missionary with you. Those precious times were the breeding ground for today's accomplishment.

Rev. Demond Joe Decker: You, my friend, have adapted prayer as life itself. Nothing in this world would replace those wonderful times we had together praying on the phone and during my time with you in Italy.

Pastor Allwyn Dmello: You are one of the many pastors who has placed so much value on the ministry of prayer. Thanks for your unbreakable passion for the Kingdom of God.

Apostle David Moses: You are a friend who understands what it takes to live without. Our experience together in Togo can never be forgotten. Thanks for not giving up your dream.

Pastor Dave Gibbons: Although we haven't met personally, reading through your book (*Liquid Leadership for a Third-Culture Church*) tells me of who you really are. Your book almost brought me to tears while on my trip to Italy. Without any doubt, I know your prayer-life has been a major contributor to your success.

Pastor Timothy Baldwin: Your sensitivity to the need for prayer shows that you understand it is the key to lasting revival. For this I am grateful.

Pastor Rotimi Wan: Thanks for making your testimony available for this book and for being my prayer partner.

———⚬⚬⚬———

In the end, in order for this book to come to life, it also took the work of a slew of dedicated people at Destiny Image. I extend my thanks to them for accepting this project in such an open way and a special thanks to Tracy Shuman and her team for praying through this project.

Finally, I offer resounding acknowledgment to my mom and dada, who did not allow me to die before my time. Thanks to my siblings, Kate, Victor, Glory, Ufuoma, and Charles, for making prayer your breath.

Contents

Foreword

My spiritual son, Paul Eguridu, has not only written a wonderful book about prayer, he lives a prayer-filled existence. If you have had the privilege of traveling to Nigeria in West Africa, you have likely experienced some of the "prayingest" people in the world. Having been there many times, I believe that Nigerian Christians are the "mid-wives" of the greatest prayer movement in the world. Paul is a native of Nigeria, which brought him exposure to the life of a praying minister. Other great men of God also mentored him in his early years there, imparting a spirit of intercession. This experience made the difference between a minister who prays and a man of prayer who ministers.

Paul has opened up very private parts of his very public life in this book. Most of the prayer experiences he relates are his own, not someone else's. You will find yourself believing afresh that God can—and will—answer your prayers. This is not a typical manual on how to pray. Paul has captured the heart and call of the Father to each of us who desire to see God move mountains, raise the dead, heal the sick, and provide supernaturally for all our needs according to His riches in glory! *PrayerWorks* could be the book that opens the heavens over your life and changes how you approach every situation.

You are likely to pick this book up many times after you've read it. I encourage you to use it as a tool of encouragement for your journey to become a person of prayer, not just a person who prays. Paul's stories show the difference between these two kinds of believers.

Paul has been a part of our church since 2004. The first time he came was on a Sunday morning. In the midst of a great move of God's Spirit, I called him out of the congregation (not a common practice) and asked him to lead us in prayer. Why? When I looked at him, the Lord instantly spoke and told me that this young man knew how to move Heaven through prayer! Don't put this book on a shelf. This is a must read—it could change your life!

Bishop Bart Pierce
Rock City Church
Baltimore, Maryland

Powerful Prayers

Fatigue sapping my strength, I crumpled to the floor. I had traveled to India for a five-week-long series of Gospel meetings, not realizing my hosts would book such a demanding schedule. Toward the end of my trip, preaching and teaching appointments filled my days and extended into the nights. The coordinator of my itinerary sometimes scheduled six appointments in one day—and in different cities. Some places were two or three hours apart, with crowds eagerly gathering to hear my message before I arrived.

On the last Sunday of my visit I preached five times before exhaustion overcame me. I had delivered five different messages, thanks to the Holy Spirit, who showed me unique needs that existed in each place. Now I wondered how I could possibly deliver the sixth. Pastors across this particular city had announced the meeting publicly, and the crusade drew thousands, including the chief of police. Anticipation filled the air after reports of miraculous events at other meetings circulated through the crowd.

With my strength drained, I fought a sense of dread. The thrill of seeing so many people set free, coupled with ever-present spiritual warfare, had emptied my physical and emotional reservoirs. When I tried to speak, my pitiful croaking left listeners straining to hear me. The spiritual son traveling with me, my host, and the coordinator of my schedule could easily see the exhaustion that threatened to drag me under. With just 20 minutes left before our driver was due to shuttle us to the crusade, I told everyone, "Please leave me alone. I have to have some time by myself with God."

After they left, I knelt beside my bed and anointed my head with oil. Then I prayed, applying the principle of knocking: *"Continue earnestly in prayer, being vigilant in it with thanksgiving; meanwhile praying also for us, that God would open to us a door for the word, to speak the mystery of Christ, for which I am also in chains"* (Col. 4:2-3 NKJV). As I asked for this door to open and the strength to fulfill my task, I heard a still, small voice in my spirit.

"My presence will go with you into the crusade, and I will give you rest and peace," the Spirit said, echoing the promise God made to Moses thousands of years before: *"The Lord answered, 'I Myself will go with you, and I will give you victory'"* (Exod. 33:14). When I heard this voice speaking, I knew that God had opened the door of utterance. However, I still felt as tired as when I sank to my knees. When the knock on the door sounded, I trudged into the night, wondering how I would deliver the day's final message.

God quickly showed me. The evidence of the answer to that prayer appeared when I stood before the multitudes and started to speak. The Holy Spirit had given me a word of knowledge (a prophetic word of wisdom) for the chief of police, one of several VIPs at the meeting. As I called on him to stand before the crowd, strength flowed into my body like a bolt of lightning, filling me with supernatural energy. I believed, in that moment, that I could send an army of 10,000 fleeing. *"Five of you will chase a hundred men; a hundred of you will chase ten thousand men. You will defeat your enemies and kill them with your sword"* (Lev. 26:8).

When I spoke to the police chief, I spoke to him about the thought he carried in his heart regarding his personal ambitions in the political arena. "If you run, God will be behind you and guide you through this process," I told him. After arriving at this meeting wondering how I could even deliver the message, I went on to give one of the best during that autumn of 2006. Today the testimony of God's miraculous power is still discussed in that region. People recall how the air was thick with the anointing of the Holy Spirit, which brought unity among the pastors of that city. In addition to numerous conversions, many were healed of pain and sickness or had spells of gloom and despair broken off their lives. Barren women later gave birth. After hearing what happened at the meeting, pastors and their spouses came to my hotel in the wee hours of the morning, hoping for healing, counseling, or a word of knowledge.

A Powerful Weapon

Prayer is one of the most powerful weapons God has given to His children. This is a tremendous asset; without it there is no communication link with our Father. It creates a doorway between humanity and God, exchanging human weakness for Christ's power. Prayer is designed to create an ever-increasing communion with God so believers can renew their strength and seize God's power to undo the devil's works.

Redemption through Jesus gives every believer equal access to this divine hotline. Sadly, many are not utilizing it because of a lack of understanding. Since many believers don't know how to pray, they approach God without understanding and see no fruit from their prayer lives. In Hosea 4:6 God says, *"My people are destroyed for lack of knowledge..."* (NKJV)—not a lack of prayer.

To grasp the power of prayer, it helps to look at biblical examples of great prayer warriors. The prophet Daniel prayed effectively and fruitfully because of his understanding and working knowledge of prayer. He knew what it could do. Daniel's prayer life attracted angelic visitations and brought about divine information with skill and understanding:

> *Gabriel came to me. (I had seen him in my last vi-*
> *sion.) He came flying quickly to me about the time*
> *of the evening sacrifice, while I was still praying.*
> *He taught me and said to me, "Daniel, I have come*
> *to give you wisdom and to help you understand"*
> (Daniel 9:21-22).

Gabriel went on to explain to Daniel things that were going to take place in the future and how God's people would be affected. I believe many present-day believers lack skill with and understanding of prayer. It is no wonder so many prayers go unanswered; many people fail to use the right key to open doors in the heavenly realm.

Even in the natural world, you can't use your house key to start your car, no matter how expensive the house or the car. You can fast and pray for days on end, asking God to help your house key operate your car, but it will never work because you are using the wrong key.

The same principle applies to prayer. Jesus said:

> *Ask, and it will be given to you; seek, and you will*
> *find; knock, and it will be opened to you. For every-*
> *one who asks receives, and he who seeks finds, and to*
> *him who knocks it will be opened* (Matthew 7:7-8
> NKJV).

If you want to have an effective prayer life, you need to understand asking, seeking, and knocking.

There is something in the hand of our heavenly Father that requires asking in prayer, just as there are other circumstances that require the principles of seeking or knocking. Until people know how to use the principles, or laws, of prayer, they will never experience a victorious, fruitful prayer life. There are numerous prayer warriors around the world who exhaust themselves in prayer, yet see no breakthroughs because they do not understand these concepts.

Exploring the Principles

Asking, seeking, and knocking govern the practice of prayer. Our greatest example, Jesus, knew when to ask and how to ask. He never used one law in place of another. At Lazarus' tomb, He didn't apply the principle of seeking when He raised Lazarus from the dead. He asked with authority when He called Lazarus forth from the grave:

> ...*Then Jesus looked up and said, "Father, I thank you that you heard Me. I know that you always hear Me, but I said these things because of the people here around Me. I want them to believe that you sent Me." After Jesus said this, He cried out in a loud voice, "Lazarus, come out"* (John 11:41-43).

Jesus accessed God's power to raise Lazarus from the dead after four days because He used the right key. Jesus had already applied the principle of seeking. Jesus already knew how God looked at Lazarus' death. That is why He waited two days after hearing of his friend's death. Because He knew what His Father had to say, He could declare, *"This sickness will not end in death. It is for the glory of God, to bring glory to the Son of God"* (John 11:4).

Likewise, believers should only apply the law of seeking in prayer when they want to understand God's will. If Jesus had applied the law of seeking at the tomb, He would have failed to see Lazarus arise, meaning that God would not have received any glory. In the same way, your unanswered prayers do not glorify God. You must know when to apply the laws of prayer so that you can be effective in your prayer life.

Although Jesus used the principle of asking when He prayed for Lazarus, at other times He used the principle of seeking. This law is illustrated through Scriptures such as Jeremiah 29:13 and Matthew 6:33:

> *And you will seek Me and find Me, when you search for Me with all your heart* (Jeremiah 29:13 NKJV).

> *[Jesus said]: "Seek first God's kingdom and what God wants. Then all your other needs will be met as well"* (Matthew 6:33).

Notice in these two verses that the Bible doesn't say "ask," but "seek." There are times when God hides Himself and wants us to seek Him through prayer. Use this principle when you want to know the mind of God—when you are at a crossroads and aren't sure where to turn, when it is difficult to do His will, or when you struggle to surrender your will to His.

Jesus applied this principle on the Mount of Olives before going to the cross. He prayed to God to take the cup of suffering from Him. Jesus sought God through prayer, asking whether to lay down His own will and pick up His Father's will, which meant to die. This crossroads divided the will of man from the will of God. Because of the seeking principle, Jesus surrendered His will to the will of His heavenly Father:

> *Then Jesus went about a stone's throw away from them. He kneeled down and prayed, "Father, if You are willing, take away this cup of suffering. But do what You want, not what I want"* (Luke 22:41-42).

The third principle of prayer is knocking. As Matthew 7:8 says, *"...To him who knocks it will be opened"* (NKJV). You need to pay careful attention to this principle. It is where most believers fail to experience breakthrough in their prayer life.

When He walked on this earth, Jesus told us that in the Father's house—namely, Heaven—there are many mansions: *"In My Father's house are many mansions; if it were not so, I would have told you. I go to prepare a place for you"* (John 14:2 NKJV). Every mansion in Heaven has a room; every room has a door; and every door has a key. Every room in these heavenly mansions contains different things that humans need, whether spiritual or physical. Note that only through the principle of knocking can a heavenly door open. You cannot use the principles of asking or seeking.

Knocking was the only law that Jesus did not operate in during His life on earth. That's because He is the door. As He told His followers: *"I am the door, and the person who enters through Me will be saved and will be able to come in and go out and find pasture"* (John 10:9). When the prayer of knocking touches the heart of Jesus, you can experience breakthroughs on earth. Until He opens a door in one of Heaven's rooms, you will never experience answered prayer.

In the opening of this introduction, I mentioned the door of utterance that I asked God to open during my wearying time in India. I patterned this after the apostle Paul's request from his brothers in the church at Colosse (see Col. 4:2-3). Among the rooms in God's heavenly mansions is the one of utterance. Paul asked the church in Colosse to pray and knock on the door so it would open. Then, when Paul spoke, rivers of living waters flowed from his mouth. The Holy Spirit empowered his words so they penetrated hearts and made the hearers receptive to the Gospel. You need the Holy Spirit to empower your words, so that when you speak at home or at your job, people will take your words to heart.

The Divine Link

Prayer is the strongest link between people and God, a place of divine exchange where God's strength replaces our weaknesses. You must understand the laws of prayer in order to be effective. *Out of daily communication with the Almighty God in Spirit and in truth emerges a powerful, miracle-filled life.*

God has delivered everything He had to the one who has understanding and a working knowledge of prayer. This is why you must understand *when to* ask and *how to* ask, *when to* seek and *how to* seek, *when to* knock and *how to* knock. Don't knock on the door of utterance when you are supposed to knock on the door of faith. If you do, you are knocking on the wrong door, outside the will of God. In such cases, you won't see answers.

In Acts, the early Church prayed over Paul and Barnabas and sent them on a mission to the Gentiles (see Acts 13:2-4). Their prayer must have included that a door of faith would be opened to the Gentiles to receive the Word and believe in their message. The evidence of the answer appears in Acts 14:27: *"Now when they had come and gathered the church together, they reported all that God had done with them, and that He had opened the door of faith to the Gentiles"* (NKJV).

Remember, when you want to know the mind of God concerning a situation or are at a crossroads and don't know where to turn, apply the law of seeking. Once you have discovered what God wants you to have or what He wants you to do, apply the law of asking. When there is resistance and you need a breakthrough—a door to open in the heavenly realm to change things in the natural realm—apply the law of knocking.

Whatever the principle, you must persevere. Take the law of knocking. Through prayer and fasting for 21 days, Daniel knocked on the door of revelation. Although there was resistance, Daniel did not give up until he received a response from Heaven (see Dan. 10:1-14). Peter knocked on a physical door after his supernatural release from prison, thanks to the saints' continual prayers. Peter did not stop knocking at the door until the door opened and he could share about the divine intervention in his release from prison by the angel of the Lord. The story in Acts 12:1-16 concludes with these words: *"Peter continued to knock, and when they opened the door, they saw him and were amazed."*

The Value of Prayer

Throughout this book, my greatest desire is that the Holy Spirit would give you a deeper perspective on prayer and a greater appreciation for its value. I want you to understand that prayer is the greatest work to which God calls humans. I hope this book will help you gain a stronger working knowledge of what prayer can do when rightly applied. Used correctly by those who pray, this awesome tool will accomplish God's purposes on earth and destroy satan's intentions.

If twenty-first-century believers would grasp how God has called His Church to labor with Him in prayer, they would see God perform more wonders than during the days of the early Church. I don't say that with a pompous spirit, nor am I making exaggerated claims. Jesus Himself promised,

> *I tell you the truth, whoever believes in Me will do the same things that I do. Those who believe will do even greater things than these, because I am going to the Father. And if you ask for anything in My name, I will do it for you so that the Father's glory will be shown through the Son. If you ask Me for anything in My name, I will do it* (John 14:12-14).

21

As we seek to see such great wonders take place before a skeptical and unbelieving world, let us follow Christ's admonition *"that men ought always to pray, and not to faint"* (Luke 18:1 KJV). Join me as we discover the wonders that prayer can accomplish.

CHAPTER ONE

The Wonders of God's Grace

*Prayer is the medium by which God releases
His grace to human hearts.*

When Kumar walked into an upstairs bedroom at his brother-in-law's home, he had no idea he was about to meet God. The story goes back to a childhood when this son of Hindu immigrants from India learned a lot about religion, but rarely saw anyone live the truth of the Gospel.

Ironically, Kumar believed in Jesus. As a boy, he learned several Christian songs at school. When the class sang them, he sensed Christ's presence in the room. He also heard about God from classmates and two sisters who attended a parochial school. Yet Kumar never decided to follow Christ because of a series of unfavorable experiences with Christians. Over the years he had met numerous hypocrites, people who told him they believed in God, but whose actions did not match their words. Some were elders or church leaders, but he knew on the weekends they loved to visit bars or strip joints. Others loved to tell him he was going to hell; one time, some visitors to his home jumped up and down on the porch while proclaiming that message. Because of such contradictions and extremes, he never had a desire to uncover the truth. Instead, he pursued his interests in business and became an investment counselor.

Despite his disillusioning spiritual experiences, there was another reason Kumar knew Christ was real: he had seen Him answer prayers. Whether stuck in a bad financial situation or some other problem, a dozen times he had prayed and seen God respond. For years, the Lord showed him things that were going to happen in his life, a reality that finally drove him to his knees. "In November of 2002, around Thanksgiving, he said, 'You've shown me all these things. I just don't see them happening in other people's lives.'"

Still searching for the reality of authentic believers, Kumar wasn't too impressed when a friend tried to tell him about Christ. A week after that encounter, he went to his nephew's birthday party. When he went upstairs to talk to his brother-in-law and knocked on the bedroom door, nobody answered. Later, his brother-in-law told him, "We're going upstairs if you want to come."

Kumar followed. For the next three hours his brother-in-law and his in-law's brother talked to him about Christ. At first he resisted. He didn't think it was necessary to make a verbal commitment to Jesus in front of other people. He also hung back, waiting for one of those "you're going to hell" statements or other claims that would let him mentally shut down. Not that Kumar didn't care about Heaven, but he thought if God was really God, He should be the Lord over his life in the here-and-now.

"I was just waiting for them to slip up and say something along those lines, which everyone who had ever talked to me would eventually say," Kumar says. "But they never did. What was going on was when I went up the first time and knocked on the bedroom door, those guys were praying up the room. I found out later they knew this appointment with me was coming the week beforehand. As I was listening to them, I thought, 'Something's going on here, something in the Spirit, because they're not walking down the roads that would cut me off.'"

Had those relatives not prayed prior to that encounter and been obedient to the Holy Spirit's guidance that night, he is convinced that he never would have come to that decision to follow Christ. Had they been arrogant or injected their opinions into the conversation, he wouldn't have listened. Two weeks later, when he came to my church in Baltimore for the first time, it was as if he and I were long-lost brothers. He learned what I teach everyone: prayer has a tremendous impact on God and the situations of our lives. When we pray, we should do so expectantly.

Praying in Converts

Kumar's story is miraculous, but nothing new. J. Hudson Taylor, a legendary British missionary to China during the nineteenth century, told of a young man who had been called to foreign missions. Though not a skilled preacher, he knew how to seek God in prayer. One day he told a friend, "I don't see how God can use me on the field. I have no special talent."

"My brother, God wants men on the field who can pray," his friend replied. "There are too many preachers now and too few [pray-ers]."

"He went," Taylor recalled. "In his own room in the early dawn a voice was heard weeping and pleading for souls. All through the day, the shut door and the hush that prevailed made you feel like walking softly, for a soul was wrestling with God. Yet to this home, hungry souls would flock, drawn by some irresistible power. Ah, the mystery was unlocked. In the secret chamber lost souls were pleaded for and claimed. The Holy Ghost knew just where they were and sent them along."[1]

These stories describe what King Solomon wrote: *"The king's heart is in the hand of the Lord, like the rivers of water; He turns it wherever He wishes"* (Prov. 21:1 NKJV). The influence that controls the hearts of the unsaved can be likened to the kings in this verse. Many interpret it in relation to political leaders or government officials, but I think it has a broader application. Any situation contrary to your walk with God represents a king, a controlling power opposing you. Solomon is saying that the king's heart rests in your heavenly Father's hand. If you engage God in fervent prayer, He will turn the situation around. Prayer is that force that brings irresistible power, which moves the unsaved to consider the reality of Christ's sacrifice.

The Miracle of Salvation

The miracle of salvation occurs when God buys back a human soul from the slave market of sin. It is the greatest wonder any person can experience. Every other miracle people see is limited to their time on earth, but salvation follows people throughout eternity. This profound event only occurs through God's grace, as pointed out in Ephesians:

> *I mean that you have been saved by grace through believing. You did not save yourselves; it was a gift from God. It was not the result of your own efforts, so you cannot brag about it* (Ephesians 2:8-9).

This grace flows through the hand of faith. Prayer is connected to it because prayer is the expression of your faith.

Prayer, speech, and belief go hand in hand. As Paul wrote,

> *This is what the Scripture says: "The word is near you; it is in your mouth and in your heart." That is the teaching of faith that we are telling. If you declare with your mouth, "Jesus is Lord," and if you believe in your heart that God raised Jesus from the*

dead, you will be saved. We believe with our hearts, and so we are made right with God. And we declare with our mouths that we believe, and so we are saved (Romans 10:8-10).

If you believe in your heart, but do not confess with your mouth (which involves prayer), your salvation is not complete. Until you profess what you believe, you will never experience this wonderful grace. Paul understood that prayer is the force that releases God's grace into people's hearts so it can accomplish their salvation. God has made this power available to everyone who follows Christ. However, for that grace to fulfill His purpose in your life, it must flow through prayer.

There are billions of unsaved souls in the world who have not entered God's Kingdom because satan has blinded them to the truth:

If the Good News that we preach is hidden, it is hidden only to those who are lost. The devil who rules this world has blinded the minds of those who do not believe. They cannot see the light of the Good News—the Good News about the glory of Christ, who is exactly like God (2 Corinthians 4:3-4).

While the devil is responsible for the unsaved souls in our world, the Church has given the devil access to do whatever he wants with the unsaved. It is the lack of effectual, fervent prayer among Christ's followers that gives the devil permission to blind people's minds. Because of its prayerlessness, the Church bears some responsibility for the liberty satan has in multiplying his activities and controlling humans.

Since the devil especially dreads prayer from the Church, he strives to keep the saints from praying. He fears nothing from our prayerless studies, prayerless work, or prayerless religion. Satan laughs at our toil and mocks our wisdom, but when we engage in serious prayer, he trembles. Prayer is where we receive

God's grace to terminate the devil's plans for the earth. Among its many unique qualities:

PRAYER RELEASES GOD'S GRACE. As Paul wrote to the Corinthians:

> *I begged the Lord three times to take this problem away from me. But He said to me, "My grace is enough for you. When you are weak, My power is made perfect in you." So I am very happy to brag about my weaknesses. Then Christ's power can live in me* (2 Corinthians 12:8-9).

PRAYER CONVEYS GOD'S GRACE. It is the divinely appointed channel through which grace flows to human souls. If the Church will return to the basis of effectual, fervent prayer, it will see people's hearts turn toward their Creator. I have often said, "It is impossible to touch the heart of a man if you have not touched the God that created the man's heart."

PRAYER DESTROYS SATAN'S POWER. Grace destroys the powers of darkness and brings light to people's hearts so they can know the truth. Since unsaved souls lack light, the power of darkness controls them. But when light comes, darkness disappears. Such was the case with Lydia, a merchant described in Acts:

> *On the Sabbath day we went outside the city gate to the river where we thought we would find a special place for prayer. Some women had gathered there, so we sat down and talked with them. One of the listeners was a woman named Lydia from the city of Thyatira whose job was selling purple cloth. She worshiped God, and he opened her mind to pay attention to what Paul was saying. She and all the people in her house were baptized. Then she invited us to her home, saying, "If you think I am truly a believer in the Lord, then come stay in*

> *my house." And she persuaded us to stay with her* (Acts 16:13-15).

After the release of prayer, God opened Lydia's heart so she could receive His message as spoken through Paul. Prayer created the atmosphere for grace to not only be released to Lydia, but also to save her whole household.

PRAYER MOVES THE HAND THAT MOVES HUMAN HEARTS. God has admonished us to seek salvation for unsaved souls: *"If you ask Me, I will give you the nations; all the people on earth will be yours"* (Ps. 2:8). Prayer influences God to touch people. He releases His grace into their hearts, making it possible for them to receive the word of God that brings them into His Kingdom.

A God-Given Privilege

Prayer is the Church's God-given privilege for stopping satan's activity, but much of the modern Church has neglected it. The early Church prayed fervently and constantly turned back the kingdom of darkness. Prayer empowered them and sustained their spiritual fire: *"But we will give ourselves continually to prayer and to the ministry of the word"* (Acts 6:4 NKJV).

Whenever the early Church prayed, we see undeniable evidence that it touched Heaven. For example, look at what happened when Paul and Silas were thrown in jail for their preaching. At midnight they prayed and sang praises to God so loudly that the other prisoners heard them. Suddenly a great earthquake shook the jail's foundations, throwing open the doors and loosening everyone's bonds (see Acts 16:16-34).

While prayer is designed to enrich people, it affects God and moves Him to act on humans' behalf. We must remember such power when we recognize that, while salvation is for all people, not all are saved. Prayer will release the grace that brings conversion. God is not a Father Christmas who just distributes gifts to every one that comes to Him; He wants to hear the Church cry out to Him in prayer so He can release that grace that turns the hearts of people to Him.

The prophet Elijah understood the importance of prayer. When he spoke to God, he was serious and expected results: *"Lord, answer my prayer so these people will know that you, Lord, are God and that you will change their minds"* (1 Kings 18:37). If the prophet Elijah had not prayed, the hearts of the children of Israel would not have turned back to God. We would not see the evidence of an answer to his prayer in verse 39, which says that the people fell on their faces and cried out, *"The Lord is God! The Lord is God!"* While God wanted the people to turn back to Him, the Lord needed someone to pray so that grace could be released. When Elijah prayed, God accomplished His intentions.

Hearing the Truth

There is safety in the truth, which is why the devil strives to keep people from hearing and receiving it. If only the Church would pray as Jesus admonished! If we will, the Kingdom of light will inflict damage on the kingdom of darkness:

> *Then they put these men before the apostles, who prayed and laid their hands on them. The word of God was continuing to spread. The group of followers in Jerusalem increased, and a great number of the Jewish priests believed and obeyed* (Acts 6:6-7).

In Luke 10:2, when Jesus Christ told His disciples to pray that God would send laborers into the harvest fields, I believe what He meant was to ask that God would send people who will labor with God in prayer, asking Him to release the spirit of grace on others' hearts, making it possible for them to receive the Gospel of God's Kingdom.

Given this prayer request, it seems obvious that if there is a lack of prayer in the present-day Church, the Lord of the harvest cannot send forth laborers into the fields because God does not work alone. He could if He wanted, but according to His Word, He needs our prayers to accomplish His work on earth. Too many believers, and the Church as a whole, aren't experiencing the dimension of grace that brings transformation in people's lives. The Holy Spirit is that "Lord of the harvest" who will empower your prayer life. The Spirit can bring your prayers to the boiling point, enabling you to send divine vapors to Heaven. This creates an atmosphere where God's irresistible power brings souls into His Kingdom.

As you read this book, I pray the Holy Spirit will anoint you with the spirit of effectual and fervent prayer so you can win souls into God's Kingdom through prayer. Whether you are a pastor, teacher, evangelist, or church member, as I write this I am asking God to baptize you with fresh fire as you agree to labor with Him in prayer.

Today God is preparing to release an awesome grace that will transform people, neighborhoods, cities, states, and nations. It is available to anyone who will get serious about prayer. Rise up. Stop tolerating the devil's schemes in your life and the lives of your family, friends, co-workers, and others. God is committed to answer your prayers if you pray with understanding.

From here on, I will include a prayer at the end of each chapter. I hope you will take time to stop and meditate on these words:

Dear Father, I come to You today with an open heart and a willing mind, presenting my empty vessel to You. Fill me with unusual grace to become an intercessor for humanity's salvation. Holy Spirit,

I give You my tongue and ask that You use it as an instrument to create an irresistible atmosphere, drawing souls into Your Kingdom. God, I thank you for a fresh baptism of passion for prayer in my life. In Jesus' name, amen.

Endnote

1. E.M. Bounds and Harold Chadwick, *E.M. Bounds: The Classic Collection on Prayer* (Alachua, FL: Bridge-Logos Publishers, 2001), 255.

CHAPTER TWO

The Wonders of God's Visitation

Prayer is the channel to revival.

The young man who had come to see me had a haunted look in his eyes, as if he were staring over a cliff and knew he was about to plunge to his death. Facing financial ruin in his first business venture, he had been contemplating suicide because of the heartache, embarrassment, regret, and fear that stalked him day and night. He had risked his life's savings and saw no way out of certain misery. He didn't know where to go or what to say. A mutual acquaintance had brought him to my home for counseling and prayer.

The origin of his trouble started with a shady business operator in London. The young man planned to market factory overstocks—shoes, men's and women's clothing, and other items. As he flew to Great Britain from his home in Togo to inspect merchandise sources and sign an agreement, he thought he had covered all the bases. But when the first container arrived in West Africa, it was stuffed full of worthless merchandise. When he tried to contact his "partner" in London, the man had changed his phone number and mailing address, leaving no trace of his whereabouts.

As he shared his sad tale, my heart skipped a beat. I had recently started my first assignment as a missionary and found myself staring head-on at a matter of life and death. I listened intently for direction from the Holy Spirit as he talked. When he finished, I opened my mouth to pray when the Word of God suddenly filled it. The words of Micah 7:7-8 came rushing out,

> *Therefore I will look unto the Lord; I will wait for the God of my salvation: my God will hear me. Rejoice not against me, O mine enemy: when I fall, I shall arise; when I sit in darkness, the Lord shall be a light unto me* (KJV).

"The Lord will be your light," I told him when I had finished reciting this passage. "The Holy Spirit declares that all is not lost—this is the beginning of a bigger adventure. This is not the end of your life."

My words instantly caused a change in his countenance. With fresh hope dawning in his spirit, he broke into a huge smile. This marked a personal revival. After lingering at death's doorstep, he had reasons to be optimistic about the future. He saw a way where there had been no way. Two months later, I saw my words come to pass. The people who had loaned him money gave him grace, enabling him to take another loan to purchase more goods. Finding a more reliable source, he had secured another shipment and was well on his way to establishing a prosperous business.

God's Visitation

Prayer accomplishes the wonder of God's visitation known as "revival." Revival is more than an emotional sensation, dynamic sermons, or stimulating religious feelings that come rushing in, only to fade. *Revival* means "life again." Every believer in Christ who is genuinely born again is born into the life of God. As John 3:6 puts it, *"That which is born of the flesh is flesh, and that which is born of the Spirit is spirit"* (NKJV). The life of God comes into your spirit and your spirit begins to live through the Spirit within.

This is what happens during salvation. God's Spirit (breath) comes into a human's spirit and that person starts the Spirit-filled journey in the same way that Adam came to life: *"Then the Lord God took dust from the ground and formed a man from it. He breathed the breath of life into the man's nose, and the man became a living person"* (Gen. 2:7).

This life of God coming alive in you when you decide to follow Christ is supposed to grow and develop through fellowship with God in His Word and prayer. However, many believers follow an unbalanced lifestyle, allowing worldly cares, riches, and pleasures to choke off the Spirit. When that happens, God's "life" gradually withers until they no longer sense His presence. God's inner lamp sputters because there is no more oil (the Holy Spirit's anointing).

Coming alive in God is more than going to church on Sunday, hearing a good sermon, and returning home with an emotional high. Without ongoing prayer and the study of God's Word, one's spirit loses sensitivity to the Spirit of God because earthly problems overcome it: *"The worries of this life, the temptation of wealth, and many other evil desires keep the teaching from growing and producing fruit in their lives"* (Mark 4:19).

Evergreen Christians

During winter almost every plant loses its leaves. They look as if they are dead because growing conditions withdraw. This is an example of a believer who allows circumstances to drain the very life of God from him or her. Such people only sense the Spirit at church. After that, it is all over until next Sunday. They have no quality time with God. Their prayer lives are empty and do not attract God's attention. Is this you? Then you need revival. Rise up and come out of your winter season.

Your goal is to become like another group of believers who have decided to not allow life's setbacks to rob them of God's presence. These believers stay fresh year-round because they stay close to the river of life through constant fellowship with God. They are the kind of believers described in the Psalms:

> *Happy are those who don't listen to the wicked, who don't go where sinners go, who don't do what evil people do. They love the Lord's teachings, and they think about those teachings day and night. They are strong, like a tree planted by a river. The tree produces fruit in season, and its leaves don't die. Everything they do will succeed* (Psalm 1:1-3).

This passage describes the kind of person God the Creator expects you to be. I call it an "evergreen Christian." Evergreen plants retain their flourishing appearance throughout the year. The atmosphere does not change their ability to remain green year-round because that is how they are created. Winter does not cause their color to fade or make their leaves drop. God wants His Church to remain like the evergreen, to retain His Spirit in a world of wickedness.

Daniel remained like the evergreen because consistent, effectual prayer constantly renewed God's life within him. His faith became so contagious in the kingdom of Babylon that King Darius spread it everywhere:

> *Then King Darius wrote a letter to all people and all nations, to those who spoke every language in the world: "I wish you great peace and wealth. I am making a new law for people in every part of my kingdom. All of you must fear and respect the God of Daniel. Daniel's God is the living God; he lives*

> *forever. His kingdom will never be destroyed, and his*
> *rule will never end"* (Daniel 6:25-26).

This is the essence of revival. God wants to reveal His life to the world. He is looking for willing vessels who will allow themselves to serve as channels for God's life and allow Him to flow to a dying world bound by the powers of darkness. Will you be one of those vessels? If so, recognize that prayer is not optional. It is a vital responsibility. That is why Jesus, after warning of the last days, told His followers to always pray and never lose hope (see Luke 18:1). In First Thessalonians 5:17, Paul told the Church to pray without ceasing. This habit of constant prayer is why the first-century Church retained God's fire and an evergreen nature.

Whenever these early believers prayed, there were undeniable proofs that they touched Heaven (see Acts 4:23-31). When your soul is genuinely revived, prayer becomes a lifestyle. I hope that if you are reading this book and sense that the Holy Spirit is speaking to you, you will pay attention. Is He revealing how badly your prayer life has deteriorated, that it is at the point of dragging? This shows that your spirit is drooping and you are drifting further away from God. A consistent, effectual prayer life is the way to maintain and sustain God's life in you and become a witness for Him.

God's presence is not as evident in our world today as in New Testament times. It's not because miracles have passed away or God is no long revealing Himself to His people, but because prayer has been shorn of its effectiveness and power. God's greatest desire is to see His Church become what He formed it to be: a light in the darkness and a Body that walks in dominion in every area. While many in the Church wait for God to revive them, God is waiting for the Church to get into His divine "labor room" and passionately engage Him in prayer. Once the Church does, He can send the rain of His presence into the hearts of men and women in every nation.

Vapor and Rain

Though commonly portrayed as a patient man who endured suffering, the dimension of Job's faith is much richer. He understood God's power in a way that most modern people fail to grasp.

> *God is so great, greater than we can understand! No one knows how old He is. He evaporates the drops of water from the earth and turns them into rain. The rain then pours down from the clouds, and showers fall on people* (Job 36:26-28).

Just as most plants look dead during winter but come alive again during spring because of rain, so are dry believers refreshed by the rain of God's presence. His life shines forth through them. In the Bible, rain represents the anointing of the Holy Spirit, which is the life of God known as revival, but this rain only comes through the channel of prayer. It is the degree of vapor that will determine the measure of rain. Small vapor means modest rain. Big vapor sparks a downpour. Without vapor to make dark clouds, there can't be much moisture. When God's people engage in earnest, intense prayer, the heavens will darken and send rain over the earth, as outlined in Ecclesiastes 11:3. There are nations and people who are already experiencing a dimension of revival because intercessors in these nations—for example, Nigeria, South Korea, Uganda, Fiji, China, Cambodia, and Indonesia—have invested prayer to form the dark clouds that bring rain.

To see more of God's rain, we need to see more prayer. I gained an appreciation for the parallels between vapor and rain, and prayer and revival, in my homeland. Born in an area of Nigeria surrounded by rivers, I saw how the moisture that constantly sends up vapors when there is considerable sunshine gradually forms dark clouds, bringing rain even during the dry season. Because of the conditions in this region, this part of Nigeria experiences more rain than anywhere else in the country.

You can experience some level of personal revival even as you read this book, but there is also national revival that involves uncommon, intense, corporate intercessory prayer. It will come from believers with a strong desire to see their cities and nations turn to God. Genuine revival affects almost every area of society.

Many churches are praying and seeking God for revival. Some have grown frustrated over waiting, to the point of giving up. They shouldn't. Prayer will cause revival to fall into our churches and bring awakening. If prayer moves God to send His presence, it must first move the people who are praying. Heartfelt prayer is the prayer that finds a thoroughfare to Heaven and forms dark rainclouds. For inspiration, we can look to an Old Testament prophet:

> *Elijah was a human being just like us. He prayed that it would not rain, and it did not rain on the land for three and a half years! Then Elijah prayed again, and the rain came down from the sky, and the land produced crops again* (James 5:17-18).

The results of that heartfelt prayer are recorded in First Kings 18:42-44:

> *So King Ahab went to eat and drink. At the same time Elijah climbed to the top of Mount Carmel, where he bent down to the ground with his head between his knees. Then Elijah said to his servant, "Go and look toward the sea." The servant went and looked. "I see nothing," he said. Elijah told him to*

go and look again. This happened seven times. The seventh time, the servant said, "I see a small cloud, the size of a human fist, coming from the sea." Elijah told the servant, "Go to Ahab and tell him to get his chariot ready and go home now. Otherwise, the rain will stop him."

Elijah was not involved in guesswork when he went to the top of the mountain to pray—he engaged in serious work and poured out his heart to God. He was prepared to stay there until the answer came. He kept sending his servant to check and see if the vapor of prayer had gathered enough rain. The seventh time, the sign came and the earth yielded her increase. May the Holy Spirit help you to enter into heartfelt prayer that will lead to a season of fruitfulness.

Remember, God responds to prayers coming from a passionate and focused heart. It is not what you are saying that moves God, but what you speak from your heart that makes your prayer effectual and produces results. While revival is a sovereign act of the Holy Spirit, God channels it to humans because of prayer. Persistent, continual prayer will bring the Holy Spirit upon the earth, just as it did at Pentecost. The wonders of God's visitation have not ceased: *"Ask the Lord for rain during the springtime rains. The Lord is the one who makes the clouds. He sends the showers and gives everyone green fields"* (Zech. 10:1).

Seeing a modern-day revival will take men and women who know how to pray and can move God to take hold of earth's affairs, putting life and power into the Church and its machinery. The Church does not need more money, more educated men or women, better organization, or better activities. It needs people who can pray down the Kingdom of God on earth, as Christ instructed: *"Your kingdom come. Your will be done on earth as it is in heaven"* (Matt. 6:10 NKJV).

The Greatest Revival

The revival in Wales from 1903 to 1904 represents the greatest revival in the history of the Church. God brought revival through a coal miner, Evan Roberts, who didn't engage in any work for more than seven years so he could devote himself to prayer. God used his prayers as the channel for revival.[1] Without it, that great revival would not be part of Church history. A century later, God still wants to visit His people so His people can reveal Him to the world.

Indeed, God's desire to visit His people goes back thousands of years to the days of the prophet Ezra, who wrote, on behalf of God,

> *I may stop the sky from sending rain. I may command the locusts to destroy the land. I may send sicknesses to My people. Then if My people, who are called by My name, will humble themselves, if they will pray and seek Me and stop their evil ways, I will hear them from heaven. I will forgive their sin, and I will heal their land"* (2 Chronicles 7:13-14).

When God's people humble themselves and pray with repentant hearts, God will send revival. Sin blocks the channel of God's life flowing into the Church, but this passage shows that when believers come into genuine, heart-moving prayer, Heaven will release God's righteousness and the earth will bring forth His fruit. This power will push back wickedness and darkness and shine God's light into the hearts of men and women.

This was the case with the people of Nineveh, a moving story told in Jonah 3:1-10. This marked a national revival that touched everybody and every thing. Even the animals fasted and prayed after Jonah warned, *"Every person and animal should be covered with rough cloth, and people should cry loudly to God. Everyone must turn away from evil living and stop doing harm all the time"* (Jon. 3:8).

Revival marks God's Spirit coming to infuse His life into the spirits of people. It is as if God "came to town." Because of the creature's invitation, the Creator visits His people. This powerful visitation reorders the natural world. It affects everything, including people's social, economic, and political lives. People experience the scent of God's manifest presence. With this awakening, holy fear falls upon the land. How we need this kind of experience today!

Two Dimensions of Revival

Revival has two dimensions, which are determined by the prayers of God's people:

1. The Shower Dimension

The shower dimension changes a group of people. It is a personal revival that transforms individuals, making them look like "people going to Heaven." The prophet Isaiah gave us a picture of this first dimension of revival: *"I will pour out water for the thirsty land and make streams flow on dry land. I will pour out My Spirit into your children and My blessing on your descendants"* (Isa. 44:3).

2. The Flood Dimension

The other dimension is the flood revival, which transforms cities and nations. It makes people look like "people coming from Heaven." Moses experienced this dimension after camping with God for 40 days and nights on Mount Sinai (see Exod. 34:28-30). If God's people will enter into intense, earnest, corporate prayer, the floodgates of His presence will open, creating a spiritual tsunami across the nations of the world. God did it before and wants to do it again.

Pray this prayer:

Oh Lord, I recognize how frozen Your life within me has become. Today I give You permission to set my heart on fire again. Transform my life into a channel for Your life to flow through to a dying world lost in sin. I thank You for reviving me again. In Jesus' name, amen.

Endnote

1. "The Welsh Revival," see http://www.welshrevival.com/, (accessed April 14, 2010).

CHAPTER THREE

The Wonders of Divine Freedom

*Prayer is the power that sets the captives and the
afflicted free.*

Prayer is one of God's vital solutions for human affliction. I
think of it as the Holy Ghost's prescription for deliverance from
captivity. I saw this on a trip to India in 2006. A woman came
to see me. She was a teacher at Benson High School, the school
operated by one of my spiritual sons, who hosted my visit. She
told me about her concern for her brother, then under mental
torment by the devil.

As I listened to her, the Holy Spirit gave me directions on
how to pray for the situation. I was holding a partially full glass
of water, which I had started drinking before she came to the
school office. The Holy Spirit whispered, "Pray over the glass
of water in your hand. Give it to this lady and tell her to go
home, where her brother lives, and sprinkle the water all over
the room and her brother."

When she finished describing the situation and asked for prayer, I related the instructions the Holy Spirit had given me, prayed over the glass, and handed it to her. She agreed to follow my instructions. Later, my spiritual son called me, reminding me of this woman and my prayer for her and her brother. "Her brother is completely free, mentally, from demonic torment," he said. "He is helping her look for a bigger piece of property for the expansion of our school."

Glory to God! Divine freedom is a wonder that can be more fully appreciated once you have experienced captivity and affliction. What would it mean to you to be set free spiritually, emotionally, physically, or financially? Would you shout for joy, as this man and his sister did? If you are searching for release from some form of satan's oppression, remember that no one emerges from this kind of bondage without prayer.

Look at David, a man of God who had considerable experience with affliction. Psalm 61 shows his desperation at one of these moments: *"Hear my cry, O God; attend to my prayer. From the end of the earth I will cry to You, when my heart is overwhelmed; lead me to the rock that is higher than I"* (Ps. 61:1-2 NKJV). Note the phrase, *"when my heart is overwhelmed,"* which signifies how David was under the control of a spirit other than God's Spirit. We can be sure similar spirits are attacking us when we face fear, sickness, discouragement, despair, or depression. Like David, we should say, *"Lead me to the rock that is higher than I"*—that place of freedom, protection, and safety.

Stand Fast

Captivity and affliction are real because satan is real. Numerous Christians don't believe they can be under the devil's oppression. They make the mistake of thinking that once they give their lives to Christ, all their problems will end. This is one of the enemy's biggest lies. Paul told the Galatians, *"Stand fast therefore in the liberty by which Christ has made us free, and do not be entangled again with a yoke of bondage"* (Gal. 5:1 NKJV). If these yokes didn't exist, the apostle Paul wouldn't have warned about them. Satan and his agents love to use them in an attempt to entangle believers and bring them back into bondage. These yokes can be fear, pornography, lust, pride, anger, witchcraft, sickness, fornication, or many others.

This is why Paul said we must stand fast in Christ's freedom. If we don't, the enemy will take us back under his control. Thinking you can't face satanic affliction leaves you blinded and vulnerable to attack. Why else would Peter also warn in First Peter 5:8 to be sober and vigilant about the devil because he prowls around as a roaring lion, seeking victims to devour?

These two apostles were saying the same thing: If Christians think, because they have given their lives to Christ, that they can be careless and act as if the devil doesn't exist, watch out! Satan will have a heyday. Thinking salvation buys a ticket to Easy Street is dangerous. It makes Christians lose sight of what a walk of faith is all about—a spiritual war. You can't live passively, thinking you will never face any opposition. Yes, you can enjoy the freedom that Christ has purchased for you through His sacrifice. But there is a devil out there who seeks to bring you back under his control. Christianity means fighting the *"good fight of faith,"* as Paul put it in First Timothy 6:12.

Even as you read this book, the devil hopes to put forces in place to take over your marriage, your business, your mind, or your children. There are spiritual forces in the satanic womb, ready to be released to bring you into captivity or resist every move you make in your walk with God. Know that you have a greater force in your hand to fight against these satanic forces to maintain your freedom, namely, the force of prayer.

Being a Christian does not exempt you from warfare. It only gives you an advantage over the opposition. That is a winning advantage, if you are wise enough to use it. One of my favorite passages of Scripture appears in Isaiah 43:1-2:

> *Now this is what the Lord says. He created you, people of Jacob; He formed you, people of Israel. He says, "Don't be afraid, because I have saved you. I have called you by name, and you are Mine. When you pass through the waters, I will be with you. When you cross rivers, you will not drown. When you walk through fire, you will not be burned, nor will the flames hurt you."*

God was speaking to His children, guaranteeing victory in spiritual warfare. This is the same kind of assurance we find in Psalm 56:9: *"On the day I call for help, my enemies will be defeated. I know that God is on my side."* Likewise, you need to release the power of prayer! Freedom is possible, but only when you engage the enemy by crying out to God. Appealing to Him in this manner represents one of prayer's higher dimensions because it shows God that you are in a dispirited situation. God becomes tender to those who admit their helplessness.

We shouldn't let pride or human reasoning stop us from pleading as David did in the Psalms:

> *In my trouble I called to the Lord. I cried out to my God for help. From His temple He heard my voice; my call for help reached His ears. The earth trembled and shook...He saved me from my powerful enemies, from those who hated me, because they were too strong for me* (Psalm 18:6-7,17).

This Scripture shows how crying out to God when you are under affliction makes God tender and attracts His urgent attention, which includes stirring His anger toward your enemies. Not enough Christians come into this dimension, instead remaining passive about their problems. I've heard people sigh, "Well, all I can do is pray. If God wants to bring me out of this situation, He will bring me out. There's nothing I can do." Embracing this kind of outlook generally results in praying tepid prayers, said with little faith or fervor—and often, few results. Instead of crying out to God and expecting answers, they conclude that the situation is God's will for them or that He is trying to teach them something.

Learn From Jacob

The biblical story of Jacob wrestling with God at Peniel is fascinating because it shows that you sometimes need to wrestle with God in prayer to come out of enemy captivity:

> *So Jacob was alone, and a man came and wrestled with him until the sun came up. When the man saw He could not defeat Jacob, He struck Jacob's hip and put it out of joint. Then He said to Jacob, "Let Me go. The sun is coming up." But Jacob said, "I will let You go if You will bless me." The man said to him, "What is your name?" And he answered, "Jacob." Then the man said, "Your name will no longer be Jacob. Your name will now be Israel, because you have wrestled with God and with people, and you have won." Then Jacob asked Him, "Please tell me Your name." But the man said, "Why do you ask My name?" Then He blessed Jacob there* (Genesis 32:24-29).

This story demonstrates Jacob's persistence. Even when God threw his thigh out of joint, Jacob would not give up. He held on tight. This was a divine appointment, an opportunity to build intimacy with God. As Jacob wrestled with this man—whom scholars believe was God—he gained a deeper understanding of, and appreciation for, His nature. This kind of all-out effort to grasp hold of the Lord is a picture of what God expects from your prayer life. (You will learn more about this story in Chapter 12, "The Wonder of Divine Intimacy.")

Jacob received God's blessing and a new name only after he wrestled and prevailed. Believers taken captive and afflicted by the devil will only find freedom when they engage themselves and connect with God's power through prayer so they, too, can prevail. As Jesus said in John 8:32, *"Then you will know the truth, and the truth will make you free."* This statement is a key to freedom, but until you know the truth by understanding and applying it, you will never experience freedom.

We need to seek out God with faith and confidence that He will answer. We cannot afford to be like the young woman in an old African proverb. This woman received a jug of water before setting out for a long journey across the desert. Before leaving, her mistress told her, "Don't allow the water in the jug to run dry. Before it runs out, you will find a spring in the desert. It will bring forth water, but only after you finally pour out the last of the water left in your bottle into this dry spring."

The young woman set out, knowing the secret to survival for this dangerous trip. However, as she crossed the desert and the water in her jug ran low, she started to doubt what she had heard. Suddenly, just as her mistress had promised, she came upon a dry spring. The young woman stood before it and stared, deep in thought. She wondered how in the world the few drops of water left in her jug could make this dry spring bring forth water that could sustain her for the rest of her journey. After waiting for a while, she decided to ignore her mistress' instructions.

"It just doesn't make any sense," she said.

Turning the jug up because she was already quite thirsty, she drank the last of the water left inside. Then she turned and resumed her journey across this massive desert—only to die of thirst many days later. This young woman knew the truth and understood how to apply it, but never applied it.

You may exclaim, "How foolish this young woman was! What was wrong with her?" Yet that is the case with so many Christians. They would rather live in defeat and poverty, trusting in their senses instead of the Word of God, which tells them to always pray. I hope that as you read this book, the Holy Spirit will provoke a deep desire and hunger in you to seek God in prayer, no matter what circumstances you face.

The Chains Fell Away

The early disciples understood the role prayer played in bringing about freedom from the devil's attacks. They experienced God's prayer-inspired power in action after Herod apprehended the apostle Peter. The following is the account of the freedom that comes through prayer:

> *So Peter was kept in jail, but the church prayed earnestly to God for him. The night before Herod was to bring him to trial, Peter was sleeping between two soldiers, bound with two chains. Other soldiers were guarding the door of the jail. Suddenly, an angel of the Lord stood there, and a light shined in the cell. The angel struck Peter on the side and woke him up. "Hurry! Get up!" the angel said. And the chains fell off Peter's hands. Then the angel told him, "Get dressed and put on your sandals." And Peter did. Then the angel said, "Put on your coat and follow me."*
>
> *They went past the first and second guards and came to the iron gate that separated them from the city. The gate opened by itself for them, and they went*

through it. When they had walked down one street, the angel suddenly left him.

Then Peter realized what had happened. He thought, "Now I know that the Lord really sent His angel to me. He rescued me from Herod and from all the things the people thought would happen" (Acts 12:5-8;10-11).

Herod's evil plans would have prevailed, except that the Church prayed with tenacity. Prayer released the angels, who act as our security agents and who excel in strength (see Ps. 103:20), to free Peter and ward off his enemy, even to the point of releasing him from jail. If you are in a similar place of trouble, follow the advice of James:

Is anyone among you suffering? Let him pray. Is anyone cheerful? Let him sing psalms. Is anyone among you sick? Let him call for the elders of the church, and let them pray over him, anointing him with oil in the name of the Lord (James 5:13-14 NKJV).

There are angels waiting for you to cry out to God so He will release them to fight your battles. They are God's firefighters—a divine rescue corps. Their job is to rescue believers under any form of captivity. In his book, *Answered Prayer*, legendary nineteenth-century prayer warrior Edward Bounds wrote that "there is no tear that prayer cannot wipe away or dry up. There is no depression of spirits that it cannot relieve and elevate. There is no despair that it cannot dispel."[1]

Anyone tormented, troubled, depressed, or controlled by an unholy behavior should pray for deliverance. If you want to see a yoke on your life broken, you must pray. You are called to live under the Holy Spirit's influence and power, not the devil's. Prayer frees you from the enemy's schemes and afflictions. Prayer is the key that opens the door of the glorious inheritance you possess through Christ. Only those who pray will see the fulfillment of God's Word in their lives.

This truth is illustrated by the children of Israel, who were slaves in Egypt for 430 years. God sent them help after He heard their cries in prayer. As He was talking to Moses in the desert, He said,

> *I have seen the troubles My people have suffered in Egypt, and I have heard their cries when the Egyptian slave masters hurt them. I am concerned about their pain, and I have come down to save them from the Egyptians. I will bring them out of that land and lead them to a good land with lots of room—a fertile land. It is the land of the Canaanites, Hittites, Amorites, Perizzites, Hivites, and Jebusites* (Exodus 3:7-8).

Before God renamed Abram "Abraham," He promised that his descendants (Israel) would be strangers in Egypt and under affliction for 400 years (see Gen. 15:13). So why did their bondage last 30 years longer? I believe those extra years were the result of a lack of prayer. Even though He has the power and can do anything He wants, God has told us that He does not work alone. He has given us a wonderful privilege called prayer, which is the tool He uses to carry out His plans and purposes on earth. If you sit, passive, while waiting for God to deliver you without coming into agreement with Him in prayer, you will remain in captivity. Prayer is the power that brings freedom.

Pray this prayer:

Father, I am so thankful that You are interested in setting me free from every form of captivity and affliction in my life. I passionately cry out to You for deliverance from all negative situations that are holding me back. I will not be passive in my prayer life any longer. Help me to take this privilege seriously. In Jesus' name, amen.

Endnote

1. E.M. Bounds, *Answered Prayer* (New Kensington, PA: Whitaker House, 1994), 46.

CHAPTER FOUR

The Wonders of Deliverance

Prayer is the voice that revokes generational curses.

I love to visit my tailor, a gregarious man from the Ivory Coast, a French-speaking nation in West Africa. One day in February 2005, I stopped in to pick up some clothes, only to discover he wasn't quite finished with my order. As I waited in his office, I noticed a woman staring at me. The woman appeared to be in her late thirties. After finding out why I was waiting for the tailor, she asked if I was a man of God.

"I think so," I said, grinning.

As we chatted, I learned that they, too, were from the Ivory Coast. Suddenly in the middle of our conversation I sensed the Holy Spirit saying, "Ask this woman, 'Are you married?'" When I repeated those words out loud, she looked down as she shook her head "no."

The Spirit whispered, "Ask her: 'Why are you not married?'"

When I repeated that, she said in her halting English, "Why do you say that? I can't find someone to marry me."

As soon as she spoke those words, I felt as if the Holy Spirit had opened my eyes with a supernatural vision. It could be compared to the kind Elisha had when Israel was at war with Aram and the prophet could see the horses and chariots of fire God sent to defend Israel (see 2 Kings 6:17). I saw a dark veil covering this woman's face and recognized that a generational curse had prevented her from finding a husband. I told her the Holy Spirit had given me a word of knowledge about her situation and opened a chapter of her life to me. Telling her that I sensed that a curse had touched her, I mentioned how something had always intervened to halt her marriage plans.

"Is this what happened?" I asked.

"Yes," she said, her eyes growing wide. "How did you know?"

"Pray for her and break the curse," the Spirit instructed.

When I started to speak, the words of Psalm 124:8 flowed from my lips, *"Our help is in the name of the Lord, who made heaven and earth"* (KJV). Then I said, "The curse is broken" and prayed with her. As I did, the Spirit told me to wash her feet with water, anoint her head with oil, and tell her, "The blessing of the Lord will come. Before the year is over, you are going to be married."

Though I did that, over the next several weeks I forgot about that encounter. Then, eight months later, I ran into my tailor one afternoon at a shopping mall.

"Where have you been?" he said, smiling.

"I've been busy," I replied. "In fact, I don't have much time to talk right now. I'm getting ready to leave on a trip overseas."

"Do you remember the lady you prayed for in my office?" he asked.

After he described the situation and the woman's concern over not being able to find a husband, I nodded, "Now I do, but I had forgotten about it."

"The lady is going to get married!" he exclaimed, a wide grin returning to his face. "They've been looking for you. They want you to be in the wedding."

Breaking into a shout, I screamed, "Praise the Lord!"

After calming down, I said, "Wait a minute. The week of the wedding I'm going to a conference in London. I've already booked my ticket."

Although I had to miss the wedding, that woman's breakthrough remains a highlight of my years in ministry. When God overcomes a generational curse, its power has ended—forever.

Blocking the Blessings

Generational curses can block the blessings of God in one's life. What are they? They are curses passed down to someone through his or her family blood line. It represents an inheritance that comes through natural birth, just as you receive a monetary inheritance after the death of your father or mother. What I'm about to share is something I have observed with various people I have ministered to over the years.

Just as generational blessings are real, the same is true of generational curses. This reality appears in Scripture several times, such as when the children of Israel went into captivity in Babylon because of the sins of their parents. In Isaiah 5:13, the prophet wrote, *"So My people will be captured and taken away, because they don't really know Me. All the great people will die of hunger, and the common people will die of thirst."* Later, when he wrote the book of Lamentations, Jeremiah sighed,

> *Remember, Lord, what happened to us. Look and see our disgrace. Our land has been turned over to strangers; our houses have been given to foreigners.... Our ancestors sinned against You, but they are gone; now we suffer because of their sins* (Lamentations 5:1-2,7).

The latter Scripture explains how you can inherit generational curses the same way you inherit blessings. A lack of knowledge about this can keep you from receiving your divine inheritance from God. Many believers suffer because of their parents' sins and remain in that state because of a lack of knowledge, not the devil. They are like the young African who used all his savings to buy a ticket to America. On the ship, he felt famished, particularly as he watched people going to the dining room to eat. Lacking any money for food, he didn't follow. Finally, he decided to eat and take whatever punishment the staff administered. After his meal, he waited for the waiter to bring his bill. When none came, he summoned the courage to ask what he owed.

"Nothing" the waiter replied, "the cost of food was included in your ticket."

This young man suffered hunger because he didn't know his rights. There are so many believers in the same position. God has given them the power of prayer to revoke curses and release God's blessings. While curses are blessing blockers, the Bible promises freedom:

> *Christ took away the curse the law put on us. He changed places with us and put Himself under that curse. It is written in the Scriptures, "Anyone whose body is displayed on a tree is cursed." Christ did this*

> *so that God's blessing promised to Abraham might come through Jesus Christ to those who are not Jews. Jesus died so that by our believing we could receive the Spirit that God promised* (Galatians 3:13-14).

Christ removed the curse so the blessing promised to Abraham can flow to you. The cross is where every curse is dealt with and can be converted into a blessing. However, this only happens through prayer. Too many believers suffer under generational curses of poverty, sickness, unstable marriages, untimely death, barrenness, or depression, to name a few. Although they do everything a good Christian should, such as attending church, tithing, and being involved in church activities, they cannot rise above their situations. A curse is responsible. The iniquity of their forefathers can make people prey in the hands of the devil. As Isaiah wrote when Israel's people were disobedient, *"Prepare to kill his children, because their father is guilty. They will never again take control of the earth; they will never again fill the world with their cities"* (Isa. 14:21).

The sins of your ancestors can keep you from rising to the level God has prepared for you and prevent you from entering your Promised Land. In the same way that you can't drive fast on a foggy day because of limited visibility, generational curses are like a spiritual fog covering your pathway. There are some generational iniquities that can affect behavioral patterns, such as anger or sexual perversion. If the latter operates in someone's life, that person will crave sexual relations. Even married believers can struggle with an uncontrollable sex drive. They don't know why, yet they continually lust after another person's spouse or other attractive people.

This was the case with King David, whose lust cost him fellowship with the Lord for a period of time. This problem connects to the manner in which he was conceived. Look at the confession in Psalm 51:5, which David wrote after Nathan confronted him over his illicit affair with Bathsheba: *"I was brought into this world in sin. In sin my mother gave birth to me."* Bible scholars believe David was born out of wedlock—his father, Jesse, did not legally marry David's mother. More evidence for this view exists in another of David's prayers:

> *Do not turn away from me. Do not turn Your servant away in anger; You have helped me. Do not push me away or leave me alone, God, my Savior. If my father and mother leave me, the Lord will take me in* (Psalm 27:9-10).

These Scriptures show the likelihood that David bore the scar of generational iniquity. He was the youngest of Jesse's eight sons. On the day Samuel anointed David as king of Israel, his father forgot about him as he was out tending his sheep. Jesse didn't consider that the Lord could choose him to rule over Israel, partially because of his youth, but also because of the circumstances of David's birth. (You can read the full story in First Samuel 16:1-13.)

Despite his elevation to the highest position in Israel, David continued to struggle with the curse brought on by his father's sexual perversion. Even though he was a great warrior and a man after God's own heart, he fell into the same "unholy behavior" by committing adultery with Uriah's wife (see 2 Sam. 11:1-27). Can you relate to David's battle? Can you appreciate why you struggle with unholy character traits that look impossible to get rid of, even with your strong willpower? If the root is bad, the fruit will be bad. Go to the root of the situation in your life and deal with it, and you will see the fruit become good.

Go to the Source

After Nathan exposed David's wrongdoing, the king went to the source of his problem with sexual sin. A close look at

David's prayer in Psalm 51 shows that he identified the source of his behavior. After David dealt with the situation, there is no record of his adulterous sin repeating itself. This shows that you can't get bitter water from a sweet fountain, or vice versa. As James says,

> *Do good and bad water flow from the same spring? My brothers and sisters, can a fig tree make olives, or can a grapevine make figs? No! And a well full of salty water cannot give good water* (James 3:11-12).

Another example of the inability to mix bitter and sweet predates David. Jericho came under a curse after Joshua conquered the city en route to the Promised Land:

> *Joshua made this oath: "Anyone who tries to rebuild this city of Jericho will be cursed by the Lord. The one who lays the foundation of this city will lose his oldest son, and the one who sets up the gates will lose his youngest son"* (Joshua 6:26).

These words went into effect over the land, turning the water bitter and the ground unfruitful.

However, the prophet Elisha later dealt with this situation after Elijah went to Heaven and Elisha inherited a double portion of the Holy Spirit that had been on Elijah.

> *The people of the city said to Elisha, "Look, master, this city is a nice place to live as you can see. But the water is so bad the land cannot grow crops." Elisha said, "Bring me a new bowl and put salt in it." So they brought it to him. Then he went out to the spring and threw the salt in it. He said, "This is what the Lord says: 'I have healed this water. From now on it won't cause death, and it won't keep the land from*

*growing crops.'" So the water has been healed to this
day just as Elisha had said* (2 Kings 2:19-22).

After Elisha corrected the situation and revoked the curse
over Jericho, there is no record that the land experienced
the same trouble again. This is because prayer is the voice
that revokes generational curses and transforms them into a
blessing. This is the wonder of deliverance: Prayer changes a
barren land to fruitful. It goes deep into the hidden part of
a man or woman, digging out the impurities that trouble the
soul and filling it up with the spirit of righteousness. Prayer is
a miracle salve for the intercessor, a vast power that God placed
in the hands of His saints. It accomplishes great purposes and
achieves uncommon results. It is capable of proving its power
through those who pray.

You don't need to remain under the burden of a generational
curse. The victory of the cross is calling you to engage God in
concentrated prayer in order to release His power to break the
curse over your life. Be like David, who proclaimed, *"God, You
will be praised in Jerusalem. We will keep our promises to You.
You hear our prayers. All people will come to You"* (Ps. 65:1-2).
Those who pray get God's attention and experience the power
that destroys the yoke of sin. Generational curses are as real as
generational blessings, but only those who employ prayer will
triumph.

Moses put prayer to the test when he interceded for Israel
and God pardoned them:

> *"So show Your strength now, Lord. Do what You
> said: 'The Lord doesn't become angry quickly, but
> He has great love. He forgives sin and law breaking.
> But the Lord never forgets to punish guilty people.
> When parents sin, He will also punish their children,
> their grandchildren, their great-grandchildren, and*

> *their great-great-grandchildren.' By Your great love,*
> *forgive these people's sin, just as You have forgiven*
> *them from the time they left Egypt until now." The*
> *Lord answered, "I have forgiven them as you asked"*
> (Numbers 14:17-20).

Moses turned God away from His plan to wipe out Israel and rebuild a new nation with the prophet at the center. His prayer revoked the curse that God intended to send. Alas, how humans' unbelief has limited God's power to work through prayer! What limitations have you placed on God because of prayerlessness? Prayerlessness does more damage to your destiny than you realize.

The Call to Prayer

Prayer is an inexhaustible voice that reaches anywhere and covers the needs, desires, and wants of humanity. Look at a few examples of Christ's promises regarding prayer:

> *I tell you the truth, you can say to this mountain,*
> *"Go, fall into the sea." And if you have no doubts in*
> *your mind and believe that what you say will happen,*
> *God will do it for you. So I tell you to believe that you*
> *have received the things you ask for in prayer, and*
> *God will give them to you* (Mark 11:23-24).

> *If you ask Me for anything in My name, I will do it*
> (John 14:14).

> *In that day you will not ask Me for anything. I tell*
> *you the truth, My Father will give you anything you*
> *ask for in My name. Until now you have not asked*
> *for anything in My name. Ask and you will receive,*
> *so that your joy will be the fullest possible joy* (John
> 16:23-24).

Why did the Son of God place such a strong emphasis on prayer? I believe it was so that His Father could enrich impoverished people and secure His followers a supernatural inheritance. Prayer is a life-altering matter. Only those who respond will live under an open Heaven. Such a blessing chases away curses placed on your forefathers, which you may have inherited without knowing it.

Though they may not admit it, when you observe others' actions, you may see an indication that a curse is active in their lives. Some people have access to piles of money, but can't account for how they spend it. Heavily in debt, they have no land, house, or anything to show for all the money that passes through their hands. Others don't know what to do with their lives. They wander aimlessly, investing in all kinds of businesses, but never realizing any profit from them. Some people struggle with bad habits or unconquerable shortcomings. Failed marriages, poverty, immorality, drunkenness, sickness, or anger running through their bloodlines can stem from generational curses.

If you find yourself in such a predicament, engage in a season of intense prayer. As you do this, fasting can sharpen your spiritual senses. Cry out for God's mercy to sever you from these curses. Tell Him, "Lord, I don't know the cause of this thing, but You do. Whatever I may have done through carelessness or ignorance, which has brought this reproach on my life, Lord, have mercy! Whatever may have come on me through the negative side of my bloodline, let Your grace come over me. Let the blood of Jesus Christ go to the foundation of my natural background and correct the situation." After this prayer, rely on the promise of Lamentations 3:22, *"The Lord's love never ends; His mercies never stop."*

The Four Rs of Deliverance

Every effective and productive prayer recorded in the Bible was based on the understanding of the person praying. Lack of understanding in prayer has caused a lot of unanswered prayer. In conclusion, here are four steps to release the power of prayer to revoke any curse in your own life.

1. Recognize

The first line of action in the prayer for deliverance is to identify that you have a problem and understand why it exists. You will never recover from anything plaguing your life if you don't discover its identity. After you recognize that you have a problem, you will be able to understand that something is preventing you from reaching your destiny and the cause. Then you can move to the next step.

2. Repent

This is the next point of action. Repentance means to turn away from wrongdoing, crying out to God in godly sorrow and asking Him to forgive you of your sins and to forgive the sins of your forefathers, which may have opened the door for reproach in your life. Take to heart the message of Second Corinthians 7:10: *"The kind of sorrow God wants makes people change their hearts and lives. This leads to salvation, and you cannot be sorry for that. But the kind of sorrow the world has brings death."*

Without repentance from the sins committed by your forefathers and passed down to you, you have no legal grounds to contend with God in prayer and ask Him for mercy. After turning away from these wrongs and apologizing for them, you have legal spiritual grounds on which to stand in authority and rebuke the enemy.

3. Rebuke

After recognizing the problem and repenting of it, you can rebuke the enemy who put the curse on your life. Address the situation and call it by name. If it is the spirit of anger, disappointment, failed marriage, spells, lying, or some other problem, tell the spirit behind it to back off and never return. Trust that the same power lives in you that gave Christ this kind of power: *"Jesus stood up and commanded the wind and said to the waves, 'Quiet! Be still!' Then the wind stopped, and it became completely calm"* (Mark 4:39).

4. Replace

After you have rebuked the enemy and taken him out of the way, then you can take back what he stole from you and restore it to life. Replace the curse that has been over your life with a blessing. Pray as David did after he repented of his affair with Bathsheba: *"Restore to me the joy of Your salvation, and uphold me by Your generous Spirit"* (Ps. 51:12 NKJV). This is your hour for deliverance from generational curses.

Pray this prayer:

Father God, I come to You with an open heart. I acknowledge that there may be some inherited curses from my bloodline that may have blocked fulfillment of Your plans for my life. Today I repent of the sins of my forefathers that may have opened the door for this reproach in my life. I cry out for Your mercy. Let the blood of Jesus Christ go to the foundation of my natural background and correct the situation. In Jesus' name, amen.

CHAPTER FIVE

The Wonders of God's Glory

*Prayer is the wire that connects people to
God's glory.*

An international healing evangelist lives in my homeland of Nigeria. The Lord has used this man to bring healing and deliverance to people worldwide, radiating power through his ministry. Through his hands, God has performed amazing miracles, such as the healing of a woman in the northern part of Nigeria. At a convention where he was to speak, an elderly woman in a wheelchair found him and asked, "Pray for me so I can walk. I need to walk." Then in her sixties, she had never used her feet. After gazing back at her, he asked, "Do you want a miracle or do you want prayer?"

"Both," she replied.

"God spoke to me just now and said you're to get up and walk."

"This man is crazy," she thought. "I've never walked in my life."

So she asked him, "How can I stand and walk?"

"I said get up and walk," he repeated. "No prayer for you."

What happened next amazed everyone who witnessed this exchange. That woman stood up and started dancing! At this same meeting, a man was healed of paralysis.

Those who know this evangelist tell other astonishing stories, such as a group of armed robbers who forced his driver to stop their vehicle and demanded to know if he was a man of God. After he nodded yes, one of them said, "We are going to try your God today with this vat of acid. We want you to drink it and die."

In a loud prayer, he told God, "As surely as I drink tea in the morning, so shall I drink this acid. And I trust You to keep me safe from harm."

"OK, I will drink it," he said. This happened in 1980, and he still travels the world today!

However, despite such awesome displays of power, years later one of his children lay crippled at home. One day a woman who knew the evangelist approached him at a meeting. "You call yourself a man of God," she said. "You go everywhere to preach, heal, and deliver other people, but you can't heal your own child. Now, if you are a man of God, why is your son still crippled? Can you pray to God to let that same miracle you do to others happen to your own flesh and blood?"

The woman's question stung the evangelist. It stood as a challenge to his ministry and faith. He went home and took his boy's hands in his, meditating as a holy anger welled up within. Carrying the child into his study, he locked the door and prayed, crying out, "God, you heard what this woman said. This is Your child. Reveal Your glory in his life. Heal him so that Your name will be glorified and the devil put to shame."

As he continued in earnest prayer, he reminded God of all the great miracles He done through his ministry in many nations and countless people's lives. As he prayed, the room

grew hot. God's glory came over him and the child, whom he had laid on the floor. Suddenly the boy received strength in his feet and began walking around the room. Meanwhile, the father remained face down on the floor.

Once he realized there was movement in the room, this father opened his eyes and saw his once-crippled child walking around his study. When he opened the door, the child jumped out, a sight that so surprised the evangelist's sister-in-law that she fainted. Not long after that, his wife returned from running an errand. Taking their son back to his study, he asked her, "What will you give to God if your child can walk?" She replied, "A goat."

Going back to his office, he opened the door and their child jumped out.

"I'm going to get the goat!" she cried.

Soon after, the three of them went to his father-in-law's house. He, too, was so excited to see the boy walking that he took the evangelist to his flock to give him a goat, a valued animal in this part of the world. That day brought incredible rejoicing to this family. Yet such a story sounds beyond belief to sophisticated, twenty-first-century citizens of the world. I ask: Why? It is simply one illustration of biblical history repeating itself.

We need more people today with the faith that the prophet Elisha demonstrated thousands of years ago when the Shunammite woman's son fell dead:

> *Elisha entered the room and shut the door, so only he and the boy were in the room. Then he prayed to the Lord. He went to the bed and lay on the boy, putting his mouth on the boy's mouth, his eyes on the boy's eyes, and his hands on the boy's hands. He stretched himself out on top of the boy. Soon the boy's skin became warm. Elisha turned away and walked around the room. Then he went back and put himself*

on the boy again. The boy sneezed seven times and opened his eyes (2 Kings 4:33-35).

Men and women in modern times will never see the current of God's glory flow dramatically through their lives unless they engage in passionate prayer. This great man of God from Nigeria would not have experienced the higher voltage of God's glory if he had not fervently prayed. He never would have experienced God's wonderful glory that brings restoration.

Living in the Glory

There is no better place to live than where God's glory dwells. It is magnificent when everything around you is at rest while you stay in God's glory. The place where His glory will be fully realized is the prayer closet since prayer wires the believer to His glory. You can't camp with God in prayer and not carry His presence—a promise Christ voiced in one of His most dramatic prayers for His followers: *"I have given these people the glory that You gave Me so that they can be one, just as You and I are one"* (John 17:22).

God destined humanity to show forth His glory, but satan came to dismantle it by introducing sin to the earth. Sin destroys the image of God in you: *"For all have sinned and fall short of the glory of God"* (Rom. 3:23 NKJV). When you don't know who you are, you will allow the devil to steal your glory by sinning against God. God created Adam and Eve in His image and after His likeness. But the devil hatched a scheme to persuade Adam and Eve to eat the forbidden fruit so they could be like gods. Note the distinction: God created them in His image, but the devil wanted them to become gods (with a small "g"). Because they did not know who they were, satan deceived them and they lost their privilege of carrying God's glory.

Every time you sin, you open the door for the enemy to attack God's image in you and steal your glory. Constant prayer will draw you closer to Him and keep you further away from

the world's influence. Before they fell from grace, Adam and Eve carried a higher voltage of God's glory. This glory is what Jesus, the "last Adam" referred to in First Corinthians 15:45, restored to you. Every believer has the privilege to exercise this dimension. Every believer carries a crown of glory, but it only shines forth in prayer.

Until men and women pray, they will never release God's glory in their lives. Prayer is the wire that connects you to God's glory and delivers that current to you. In your home, you may have high voltage electricity installed in your walls, but until you flick the switch, you will never see light. Fervent prayer is the switch that turns on the glory of God, making your darkest moments like noon.

Neglecting prayer hinders the manifestation of God's glory on earth. We have not because we ask not. How full of love for God and other people would you be now if only you had prayed like that man of God in Nigeria? Ask that you may experience God and reflect His glory. An aspect of prayer is asking God for something that we earnestly desire, but do not have. He has promised us answers, but we must pay close attention to discern them. They may not arrive in the manner we expect. A prayer warrior is tenacious. He or she voices urgent requests, using arguments and reminding God of His promises in His Word. They often include loud expressions following David's pattern: *"Evening and morning and at noon I will pray, and cry aloud, and He shall hear my voice"* (Ps. 55:17 NKJV).

The Labor Room

They shall not labor in vain, nor bring forth children for trouble; for they shall be the descendants of the blessed of the Lord, and their offspring with them. It shall come to pass that before they call, I will answer; and while they are still speaking, I will hear (Isaiah 65:23-24 NKJV).

The process of childbirth is a fascinating experience. Carrying a baby in her womb is glorious for a woman, but that radiates to a new level when she gives birth. These two dimensions of glory have different levels of manifestation. When a woman is pregnant she carries a visible glory. However, when she gets to the delivery (or labor) room, she must remember to push hard if she wants to see the greater dimension of her glory. *Push* is a language a pregnant woman must use to give birth.

To the believer, *push* means to pray until something happens. Spiritually, the woman is the Church, God's called-out children. God has deposited His glory in His people, but until they enter into the labor room, they will never experience the higher dimension of birthing His purposes. Nothing ever "just happens." Something makes things happen. Prayer created the dramatic revivals that we read about in Church history. These revivals were a fulfillment of the passage in Isaiah that says,

> *Before she travailed, she brought forth; before her pain came, she was delivered of a man child. Who hath heard such a thing? Who hath seen such things? Shall the earth be made to bring forth in one day? Or shall a nation be born at once? For as soon as Zion travailed, she brought forth her children* (Isaiah 66:7-8 KJV).

This Scripture shows how the travailing—the painfully difficult work—of Zion (the Church) brings forth children of the new birth in Christ. If the Church fails to labor, she will never see the manifestation of her children, who are the evidence to the world that she is not barren. Yet we see barrenness in many of today's churches because of prayerlessness. The fruitfulness of God's glory, which attracts the world to Christ, will come through prayer. If the channel of prayer is blocked, it becomes impossible for God to reveal His glory. The world is eagerly waiting to see that come to pass, as spelled out by Paul in his letter to the Romans:

> *The sufferings we have now are nothing compared to the great glory that will be shown to us. Everything God made is waiting with excitement for God to show His children's glory completely. Everything God made was changed to become useless, not by its own wish but because God wanted it and because all along there was this hope: that everything God made would be set free from ruin to have the freedom and glory that belong to God's children* (Romans 8:18-21).

God has a glory beyond what most of His children can comprehend that is just waiting to be revealed in you. This incomprehensible glory will make you shine in a world of darkness and draw others to the Gospel. Until you enter the labor room of prayer, there will be no manifestation of your glory. The world will not be delivered from the bondage of corruption and know the freedom found in Christ. I pray the Holy Spirit will lay a burden for prayer on you and drive you into the labor room, just as He did with the Lord:

> *Jesus, filled with the Holy Spirit, returned from the Jordan River. The Spirit led Jesus into the desert where the devil tempted Jesus for forty days. Jesus ate nothing during that time, and when those days were ended, He was very hungry...After the devil had tempted Jesus in every way, he left Him to wait until a better time. Jesus returned to Galilee in the power of the Holy Spirit, and stories about Him spread all through the area. He began to teach in their synagogues, and everyone praised Him* (Luke 4:1-2; 13-15).

This passage illustrates how Jesus launched his ministry in prayer and fasting. The wilderness was His prayer room, where He labored to receive the Spirit's power so He could demonstrate His Father's glory. When Jesus left the wilderness, His fame spread across the region. After 40 days, He was so bathed in prayer that He radiated God's aroma, attracting the attention of people everywhere. You will not have access to

God's glory unless you prepare in similar ways. If the Savior labored in prayer and fasting before He could manifest God's power, you must also embrace prayer to reflect your portion of God's glory.

This is why Paul told the church in Galatia, *"My little children, again I feel the pain of childbirth for you until you truly become like Christ"* (Gal. 4:19). If this apostle had to return to the labor room on behalf of this early church, should we expect to do any less? If you are prayerless, don't wait for God's glory to come on you or His anointing to rest on you. God commits Himself to those who commit themselves to effective, fervent prayer. You will have the whole of God's glory when He has the whole of your attention. Prayer secures God's presence, gifts, face, and glory. There are no shortcuts.

Turn on the Switch

The darker the night that covers the earth, the brighter is the light of God's people. But the light cannot shine gloriously if the people of God carrying the light refuse to turn on the switch so the current can flow. If God's people remain passive and at ease, God's plans to reveal His glory and draw the unreached to His Son's Kingdom will be delayed. This is why God calls on His people to stand and let His light shine through them:

> *Arise, shine; for your light has come! And the glory of the Lord is risen upon you. For behold, the darkness shall cover the earth, and deep darkness the people; but the Lord will arise over you, and His glory will be seen upon you. The Gentiles shall come to your light, and kings to the brightness of your rising* (Isaiah 60:1-3 NKJV).

God used the prophet Isaiah to warn the nation of Israel about sin and His coming judgment, which meant they would be captured by Babylon. This prophecy and warning appears in chapters 1 through 39. From chapters 40 to 59, God comforts them while they are in captivity, urging them to fast, pray, and confess their sins so salvation can come.

However, chapters 60 through 66 provide insights after Israel's release from captivity. Through the prophet, God urges them to arise and shine because His glory has risen on them. They are no longer captive. They need to arise from despondence because the world around them is going to experience deep darkness. As they go through these painful difficulties, Israel will experience God's glory. The unsaved (the Gentiles) would come to their light, searching for solutions to their problems.

The key to the manifestation of this high voltage on God's people would be when they turned on the switch so God's glory could flow through them. The same is true today. The switch will not turn on by itself. God will not turn the switch on either. Only those who are carrying the glory can turn it on and let it shine, conquering the darkness.

Nearly 2,000 years ago, John wrote, *"The Light shines in the darkness, and the darkness has not overpowered it"* (John 1:5). Darkness prevails until light emerges. Sin, sickness, wickedness, and the devil's other oppressive weapons will prevail in the world until God's people, carrying His glory, arise and turn on the switch. They must be willing to wage war, not with guns and human force, but with focused, mighty prayer: *"And from the days of John the Baptist until now the kingdom of heaven suffers violence, and the violent take it by force"* (Matt. 11:12 NKJV).

Prayerlessness and passivity about God's purposes prevent His plans from moving forward. Only the violent will take the Kingdom. Prayer is the weapon that forces the enemy to back off and give up what belongs to God's people.

Arise! That was the first word God spoke to His people after their release from captivity. The first thing you need to know in the war against the enemy of your destiny is that you must arise and switch on the light. *"Let God arise, let His enemies be scattered; let those also who hate Him flee before Him"* (Ps. 68:1 NKJV). If the Lord's enemies will not scatter until God arises, how do you think they will scatter without you arising? Stop watching things happening around you that are contrary to God's will for your life. Arise, get into effective, fervent prayer and you will see God's glory force the enemy out of your life.

When God created the earth (see Gen. 1) and darkness covered it, He didn't stand by hopelessly. He turned on the switch and light dispelled the darkness. God promised later, *"Truly, as I live, all the earth shall be filled with the glory of the Lord"* (Num. 14:21). How can this pledge come to pass when God does not live on the earth? It will happen when His people bring their commitment to a boiling point and adopt a lifestyle of prayer, like Daniel in Babylon. Daniel prayed until there was a hole in Heaven over the nation, revealing the knowledge of God to its king and people (see Dan. 2).

So, arise! God is depending on you, through your prayers, to do more than He did with Daniel during His generation. Come out of your passive attitudes about faith and let God work through your effectual, earnest prayer. Remember, you are wired to God's glory. Let the current flow through you and your spirit will receive new life.

Pray this prayer:

Oh Lord, You have called me out of sin so I can partake of Your glory. Help me to be an extension of Your glory on the earth. May Your glory shine through me to dispel darkness in the world around me. In Jesus' name, amen.

CHAPTER SIX

The Wonders of God's Life

Prayer is the believer's spiritual respirator.

As painful as it was, my youngest sister's death yielded a startling picture of the life of every believer with his or her God. Christians gain access to His life through prayer, and only with that tool can they sustain spiritual life.

Our family's tragic, unforgettable experience took place in February of 2006. When my 23-year-old sister went into the hospital to give birth to her first child, our family prepared to celebrate the arrival of another member to our clan. But in the process of her delivery, she died with the baby in her womb. Not only did she have a blood infection, she didn't receive proper medication. I knew nothing about this until I received the terrible call that every person dreads receiving. I never imagined that I would outlive her, a fact I still grieve.

When life ebbed out of my sister's body, the baby in her womb also lost his chance for life. When a baby enters the natural world, the first thing he or she must do to stay alive is inhale the oxygen circulating through the building.

Once the head emerges from the mother's womb, the baby's respiratory system must respond to nature. The babe cries as an indication that his or her respiratory system has received life. If the newborn refuses to cry or respond to the flow of oxygen, the doctor handling the delivery spanks the baby across the buttocks so the baby can use the respiratory system to breathe oxygen flowing through the lungs.

My sister's baby lived, moved, and had his being within his mother's womb. Just as her child couldn't survive without his mother, neither can Christ's followers survive spiritually without a connection to the Lord. Believers who choose to follow Christ must adopt prayer as part of their new lifestyle. It is the spiritual oxygen that causes them to breathe and live in the Spirit. Prayer is their spiritual respirator, helping them inhale this life source.

The Breath of God

Humans are three-part beings made up of body, soul, and spirit. When you are born again, your spirit gets regenerated with God's life. It comes into your spirit by faith. This life remains alive and grows as you continue to give it spiritual nutrition. Prayer is the major nutrient required for your spirit to remain lively and connected with God. Take a fish out of water and it will only survive for a short time. Take believers out of prayer and their spiritual life will fizzle. Job recognized this truth when he said, *"The Spirit of God created me, and the breath of the Almighty gave me life"* (Job 33:4).

Each of you who made a decision to follow Christ lives, moves, and has your being with Him, His Father, and the Holy Spirit. Your existence is only possible as long as you remain connected to God's divine womb and receive His free-flowing oxygen. Those who remain in constant fellowship with God in prayer will receive His life-giving substance. As Paul wrote in Acts: *"By His power we live and move and exist..."* (Acts 17:28).

If you refuse to pray or stop praying, chances are that God will allow affliction to come on you (see Ps. 119:71). Adversity is a type of spanking to any newborn Christian who refuses to respond to life. As David put it, *"In my distress I called upon the Lord, and cried out to my God; He heard my voice from His temple, and my cry came before Him, even to His ears"* (Ps. 18:6 NKJV).

Don't be like the believers who only engage in fervent prayer when they experience serious problems. This is not what God intended. He designed prayer to be His children's divine oxygen. Just as people can't live in the natural world without using their lungs to breathe, neither can they live with God unless they are hooked up to the spiritual respirator. Biographers said of legendary nineteenth-century evangelist and prayer warrior, Edward McKendree Bounds, that prayer was as natural to him as breathing. He made prayer first and foremost because he knew it to be his strongest link with God.[1]

If you wait until God allows affliction to come on you before you pray, it shows that you don't know what it means to make prayer a way of life. Granted, there can be benefits to problems; as the Psalmist wrote, *"It is good for me that I have been afflicted, that I may learn Your statutes"* (Ps. 119:71 NKJV). Still, affliction is not the best path to prayer. If that is the only time you turn to Him, it is likely that when He brings you out of the affliction, you will return to your routine. If that happens, you will neglect the ministry of prayer until God allows another affliction to strike. This was the way the children of Israel were living, crying out to God only when they were in trouble, then going back to the way they used to live.

Divine Oxygen

God's life infuses your heart as you stay in constant fellowship with Him through prayer. When you fail to pray, you are out of touch with God, cutting off divine oxygen to your spirit. The life of God within your spirit will wither. Once life dies within your spirit, you can no longer sense Him. The Word of God does not make sense to you because your spirit is out of touch with the source of life.

This is the situation in countless churches across the world today. People come to church and hear a sermon, but the message only falls on their heads instead of penetrating their hearts. Prayerlessness has cut off the divine oxygen supply to their spirits, so the life of God within their spirits fades away.

Genesis 2:7 describes God literally breathing life into Adam, raising him from the dust of the ground and a lifeless form into a living human being. Why did only this man that God made carry the life of God within him? Why didn't God put His own life into the many other creatures He created? It was because God needed someone with His nature and personality to share His love and fellowship. So God placed His Spirit in Adam to enable him to communicate with Him.

If you stop using the spiritual respirator of prayer, not only will God's Spirit within you die, you will struggle to obey His Word. This is one reason so many Christians live defeated lives. They constantly talk about what satan is doing in their lives, families, jobs, or children's lives. They have no stories of victory or testimonies of answered prayer. All they have is what they work hard to acquire, which is the kind of toil-filled existence that reaps stress and disappointment. Without God's favor, life is cruel. Being a Christian means more than going to church on Sunday. The very life of God, alive in you, makes you a true believer. Anything outside of that is nothing but a lifeless form of religion. The constant use of your spiritual respirator keeps God's breath flowing through you and keeps you alive with His presence.

When the life of God in you is no longer connected upward and you no longer look to God for the sustenance of life, you become like every other person existing without a sense of Him. While they know God lives, they cannot feel or recognize Him. When you find it difficult to obey God in every area of your life, it is because your spirit lacks proper nourishment. You are undergoing spiritual starvation.

Unquenchable Desire

The Book of Acts describes how the early disciples almost got distracted by the daily distribution of food and other ministry activities. Doing so would have diverted them from the primary reason for their walk with God and threatened the foundation of their ministry. Their attentions were gradually shifting from the ministries of prayer and teaching the Word to serving food and taking care of widows. They eventually recognized this and redirected their focus. Their giving of themselves to prayer demonstrates how they couldn't function without it. Just as you can't live without breathing in the natural, you can't live a spiritual life without praying.

The coming of the Holy Spirit and His ministry are not conditioned on a routine process and a few perfunctory prayers, but on intercession set ablaze by an unquenchable desire. Early American patriot Patrick Henry attained fame for his declaration, "Give me liberty or give me death." This great pioneer was so taken by his need for freedom that he was willing to die rather than live without liberty. As a believer, you must have that same unquenchable desire for prayer, to the point that you choose to die rather than live without God's oxygen flowing through you.

Strive to be like King David, who possessed an intense thirst for prayer. More than half the Book of Psalms is dedicated to his prayers. He constantly remained in touch with God through the effective use of his spiritual respirator. Even when his enemies came against him, he said, *"In return for my love they are my accusers, but I give myself to prayer"* (Ps. 109:4 NKJV). This declaration shows how prayer was the breath of his breathing, the thought of his thinking, the soul of his feeling, the life of his living, the sound of his hearing, and the fuel of his growth. That is what it means to give one's self to something—you are completely overtaken and consumed by it because you can't do without it. Prayer becomes the reason for your life.

The ultimate plan of God is for humans to live with Him through the spirit of prayer. This is why prayer is the most important element of a believer's life. The devil knows that a praying believer has a strong link with God and is a major threat to his kingdom. The devil dreads prayer and every person who takes prayer seriously because he understands its power. He will do everything he can to persuade you to skip praying, whatever the time of day or night.

Living Because He Lives

Prayer secures the life and breath of God. The early disciples understood this; its effective use was the secret of their power. Their unbroken connection with God enabled them to perform great miracles, signs, and wonders. They carried a constant spirit and attitude of prayer. True, their knees were not always bent or their lips not always vocal with words, but their spirits stayed in the act and communication of prayer. The spirit of prayer should rule throughout your day. As Paul declared to the Greeks in Athens, *"For in Him we live and move and have our being, as also some of your own poets have said, 'For we are also His offspring'"* (Acts 17:28 NKJV).

Likewise, you ought not to have to make any adjustments to pray. Once you understand that you are only living because God's life is flowing through you, prayer should govern every activity and work you handle. If you give yourself to prayer, God's Spirit will consistently flow through you. Nothing will be impossible for the one who lives by God's breath because it will destroy every fear, doubt, and other hindrance to faith. You will be like Peter and John who, after speaking to the priests and other rulers, demonstrated awesome power: *"And when they had prayed, the place where they were assembled together was shaken; and they were all filled with the Holy Spirit, and they spoke the word of God with boldness"* (Acts 4:31 NKJV).

When you lose the act of prayer, you die out like a fire that ceases to find new material. As fuel helps feed a burning fire, first-century believers' prayer fed their consistent commitment, releasing God's divine oxygen. It was so mighty His presence shook the building where they had gathered. The devil tried to put off the life of God in them, but they refused to pay attention. The filling of the Holy Spirit they experienced is an indication that God's fresh breath had entered them. Yet, if they hadn't prayed, they wouldn't have received that gift. Prayer fills the lungs of the believer with God's oxygen and gives you boldness, just as it did the disciples. The spirit of fear that the enemy wants to use to keep you from doing what God called you to do will fizzle away.

Prayer also keeps you in touch with the Holy Spirit, who is the One who teaches you how to pray:

> *Also, the Spirit helps us with our weakness. We do not know how to pray as we should. But the Spirit Himself speaks to God for us, even begs God for us with deep feelings that words cannot explain* (Romans 8:26).

A strong connection to the Spirit will give you access to a lifestyle of prayer, increasing your desire to pray and giving you new insights during your talks with God.

The Father gave us the Spirit to help us communicate with Him more effectively. This happened on the day of Pentecost (if you haven't already, read the second chapter of Acts) and gave the people assembled in the Upper Room a prayer language called tongues. This heavenly language came to believers to enable them to exercise their spiritual respiratory system. Using a prayer language builds up the pray-er's spirit and builds his or her spiritual life.

One caution: The Holy Spirit does not help you pray. He only comes to help when you pray. Only those who open their mouths will see the Holy Spirit empower their prayer life.

The Temple of Prayer

Jesus taught consistently about prayer. He taught His disciples how to pray in what we now call the Lord's Prayer (see Matt. 6:5-15) and erupted with holy anger when merchants turned the temple into a place focused more on business than prayer. *"Jesus said to all the people there, 'It is written in the Scriptures, "My Temple will be called a house for prayer." But you are changing it into a "hideout for robbers."'"* (Matt. 21:13).

God directed Solomon to build the temple in Jerusalem as a place where divine communication could take place. Sadly, that purpose had gotten lost amid the hustle and bustle of life (and you thought things were only hectic in the twenty-first century). Jesus reestablished that the temple is to be a place of prayer where a believer communicates with God and breathes in His life. Today, that temple is the human vessel, which is pointed out in Acts: *"The God who made the whole world and everything in it is the Lord of the land and the sky. He does not live in temples built by human hands"* (Acts 17:24).

And in his letter to the Corinthians, Paul wrote,

> *You should know that your body is a temple for the Holy Spirit who is in you. You have received the Holy*

Spirit from God. So you do not belong to yourselves,
because you were bought by God for a price. So honor
God with your bodies (1 Corinthians 6:19-20).

These Scriptures show that you are to be a temple of prayer. Every believer who has decided to follow Jesus as Lord and Savior has been bought with the price of His blood. In gratitude, each of us should be more than willing to serve as a house of prayer and demonstrate His love to the world. It is the responsibility of each believer who has the Holy Ghost inside him or her to keep the life of God flowing by making such a commitment.

Any believer who stops praying will wind up with a weak temple, one that gives no sign of life, grace, or power. So many believers have lost God's fire because of prayerlessness; they are like clanging cymbals. Prayer is also the oil that keeps the fire burning in your temple. Only this oil keeps God on fire within your spirit. If prayer fades from your life, the oil stops flowing and the fire stops burning.

As you read, the Holy Spirit may be talking to you about your lack of commitment to remain a house of prayer. If so, go to your knees in prayer and ask God to forgive you for the way you have neglected His temple. Ask the Lord to revisit you with an unquenchable desire for prayer and make you alive in His presence. If this happens, you will again experience His power and authority.

Pray this prayer:

Thank you, dear Lord, for putting Your Spirit in me so I can have fellowship with You. Help me to keep Your Spirit within me alive as I habitually stay in touch with You through prayer. Breathe into my being the atmosphere of Heaven. In Jesus' name, amen.

Endnote

1. E.M. Bounds, *Answered Prayer* (New Kensington, PA: Whitaker House, 1994).

CHAPTER SEVEN

The Wonders of Divine Authority

Prayer exercises God's authority over the earth.

No sooner had I landed at the airport in Lagos in 2006 than trouble reared its head. I wasn't too eager for a confrontation since it was my first trip to my Nigerian homeland since 2000. The friend who had come to pick me up had inadvertently parked in the wrong place. When we reached his car, a team of government officials who watched the area were getting ready to hook the vehicle to a tow truck and haul it away.

"No, please," my friend said, waving his hands. "It was my mistake. But please give us a break. I haven't seen my friend in six years."

That touched off an argument. The official kept asking for the key and my friend kept refusing to give it to him. This went on for more than 15 minutes. Finally, the Holy Spirit said, "Tell your friend, 'Why are you arguing with him?' Give me the key."

When I repeated that instruction, my friend handed me the key. Extending my hand, I said to the official, "Here's the key. I am a man of God. My friend came to pick me up. Do you want to tow the car of a man of God?"

In an instant, the ringleader of the group that had been seeking to tow my friend's car changed his expression. "We didn't know you were a man of God," he said. "Take the key. Can you pray for us?"

Since my friend was speechless, I took care of the prayer. Then we got in his car and drove away, saving ourselves the equivalent of $250. I believe that happened because when I told the officials that I was a man of God, I placed myself under His authority.

The authority of humanity, represented by the government, had to bow to God's authority. Yielding to God's authority has brought favor on my life. When Elijah faced some disbelieving guards, he said, *"If I am a man of God, then let fire come down from heaven and consume you and your fifty men"* (2 Kings 1:10 NKJV). That is what happened. Likewise, believers today who place themselves under His authority will see circumstances in their paths change.

The Power of Giving

God's authority extends to numerous areas, such as giving from one's firstfruits, a principle demonstrated throughout Scripture. Those who obey His Word in giving operate under His authority. This is demonstrated by one of my favorite stories, which I heard from a pastor in Nigeria. It concerned an American cotton farmer who fretted as he pondered the sad state of his crop. The season for harvest had arrived, but his cotton buds refused to open. It was as if they were still sewn tight in early spring. If they refused to open soon, the whole field would be wasted. Worried about this possibility, he went to see evangelist Kenneth Copeland, who was visiting the area. Copeland accepted his invitation to come see his farm and pray over his cotton.

Once he arrived, Copeland asked the man if he paid his tithes. When the farmer said he did, Copeland asked to see the checkbook from which he had paid them. Then they walked out onto the farmer's land while Copeland lifted up the checkbook. He prayed, "Lord, remember now that this is a tither and the devourer has no hold on tithers. Hear now and answer." The next day, when the farmer walked back to inspect his field, he saw that all the cotton buds had opened.[1]

I love this testimony. After this heartfelt prayer, the devil's plan to devour the farmer's harvest failed, not because Kenneth Copeland prayed, but because—as a tither—the farmer operated under God's authority. Copeland was also under God's authority, so the devil had no legal grounds to destroy the farmer's harvest.

This story illustrates why so many believers aren't seeing victory in their Christian lives. While they want to bind the devil, they are not under God's authority. Though they get involved in "spiritual warfare," they wind up exposing themselves to more of the devil's attacks. The first two chapters of Genesis relate how God created earth to be under humanity's dominion. But now the creation disobeys humanity because humans will not obey God's Word. First Kings 13:20-25 relates the story of a lion that killed a man of God because he disobeyed the Lord's instructions. However, the sixth chapter of Daniel relates how the lions didn't hurt Daniel when he was thrown into their den because of his obedience to God.

Not only must you submit to God's authority with respect to His position, you must submit to God's authority in daily life and all your circumstances. This isn't impossible, as demonstrated by the apostle Paul. Because he was under God's authority, Paul had the power to declare that Elymas, the sorcerer, would be blind for a time (see Acts 13:8-11), and Heaven backed up his command. Submit to God's authority in your daily life, listen to His voice, and obey Him in practical matters. Heaven only listens to you on earth and responds to your prayers when you are in agreement with your heavenly Father.

Walking in Dominion

While Jesus walked on this earth, He demonstrated God's power and authority to rule the earth. What He was and what He did on earth illustrate who He is and what He is doing in Heaven. Before Christ physically left the earth, He committed His earthly ministry to the Church: *"I have sent them into the world, just as You sent Me into the world"* (John 17:18).

On earth, Jesus walked in dominion. He destroyed everything that He came across that was contrary to the will of Heaven. Christ placed satan's activities here under His control. First John 3:8 makes this clear: *"The devil has been sinning since the beginning, so anyone who continues to sin belongs to the devil. The Son of God came for this purpose: to destroy the devil's work"*.

Christ dominated circumstances by exercising heavenly authority. Everywhere He went, He put the powers of darkness and demonic activities under subjection. Darkness turned to light and demons fled. What He did on earth, He is still directing from Heaven. We know this because Hebrews 13:8 says He is *"the same yesterday, today, and forever."*

Not only did He operate in divine authority, He has entrusted this task to the Church. The Master wants you and me to exercise authority. What Jesus did while on earth, He is still doing today through the Church. You must recognize your place in the ministry of Christ. God has called you to a place of power and authority. However, you must first discover your place in His kingdom and access the authority of the Kingdom to rule over the earth as God intended.

Discover Divine Placement

It is impossible to access God's authority if you don't know your place in His Kingdom. Your personal discovery of your position in Christ, who is the Head over all things, is what enables you to access this divine authority. Writing to the Church at Ephesus, Paul provided a verbal picture of what Christ has done for us and our glorious inheritance through Him.

> *I have not stopped giving thanks to God for you. I always remember you in my prayers, asking the God of our Lord Jesus Christ, the glorious Father, to give you a spirit of wisdom and revelation so that you will know him better. I pray also that you will have greater understanding in your heart so you will know the hope to which He has called us and that you will know how rich and glorious are the blessings God has promised His holy people. And you will know that God's power is very great for us who believe.*
>
> *That power is the same as the great strength God used to raise Christ from the dead and put Him at His right side in the heavenly world. God has put Christ over all rulers, authorities, powers, and kings, and every title that can be given, not only in this world but also in the next. God put everything under His power and made Him the head over everything for the church, which is Christ's body. The church is filled with Christ, and Christ fills everything in every way* (Ephesians 1:16-23).

I included the whole passage so you could read it through and allow the Holy Spirit to open your understanding and spirit to help you discover your position in God's Kingdom. There is a glorious inheritance and an exceeding power that God reserved for you to exercise through prayer. God created this world, and He owns it, not the devil. God has the right to rule this world and decided to do so through His followers, the Church. But that doesn't mean satan won't fight you each step of the way in an effort to stop you from possessing your inheritance and authority.

Jesus came to this world as the Son of God and the Son of man. He exercised the authority of God's Kingdom as both divine and human, giving us an example of how to take dominion and rule on the earth.

After Christ's death and resurrection redeemed us, He ascended to Heaven. Because He sits there, we are able to carry on spiritual warfare on earth. While His sacrifice secured your salvation, you still face a devil who wants to frustrate the works of God's Kingdom, which God created for you to accomplish. You must resist satan and claim your position as a believer. Allow this truth to sink deep into your consciousness—you have been raised with Christ and are seated together with Him in heavenly places. *"And He raised us up with Christ and gave us a seat with Him in the heavens"* (Eph. 2:6).

Christ's ascension to Heaven created a way from earth to Heaven. Jesus has opened every demonic blockage in the heavens, subjecting satan and his agents to His rule. Since we are seated with Christ, the devil is also under our feet. It is important that you allow the Holy Spirit to communicate this truth about your position in Christ into your spirit. Once you fully appreciate it, you are in position to access the authority of God's Kingdom. Through prayer, you can rule on earth as God intended.

Most Christians fail to operate in Kingdom authority activated through prayer. They try to exercise God's authority to overcome circumstances, but fail because they are not sure of their position in Christ or their identity as God's children. Once you line up with God's plan of redemption—though you are not equal with God—you are on His level. For example, look at these Scriptures:

> *I said, "You are gods, and all of you are children of the Most High"* (Psalm 82:6 NKJV).

> *Jesus answered them, "Is it not written in your law, 'I said, "You are gods"?'"* (John 10:34 NKJV)

> *The Lord said to Moses, "I have made you like God to the king of Egypt, and your brother Aaron will be like a prophet for you"* (Exodus 7:1).

Jesus walked on earth with power and authority because of His understanding of His identity as the Son of God; He knew that He was God. Moses exercised God's authority to rule and perform great signs and wonders in Egypt because he recognized that God had made him to be "a god to Pharaoh," not a dog (which is how Pharaoh looked at him). When you recognize the position God has divinely placed you in, it will give you the confidence to access God's authority through prayer.

I pray God will give you the grace to understand this. I believe many Christians don't see themselves as God's representatives on earth so they engage in warfare prayers as dogs instead of as gods. Too many prayer warriors shout and cry aloud against the devil, but lack a deep-rooted knowledge of their position in Christ. No power comes from their shouting, and the devil refuses to back away. There is nothing wrong with shouting when exercising your authority in prayer. However, before engaging in warfare, you must allow the revelation of your position with Christ in the heavens to sink deep into your consciousness. Once this happens, your shouting will produce power.

Exercise Your Authority

A young man discovered that his late father had left $50,000 for him in the Bank of America. Deciding to make a withdrawal, he went to the bank, where an officer asked him for his Social Security number. With the number, the officer accessed the account. He verified the deposit and that the young man was the rightful owner. After signing a document, the man walked out of the bank with $50,000—money he used to resolve his financial problems.

Do you see the three-step process? The man recognized he had an account with money in it, he accessed it, and he exercised the money's power. Now that I have reviewed your position in God, I want to discuss the authority He wants you to have and help you access it. It starts with Christ's promise to His disciples, *"And I will give you the keys of the kingdom of heaven, and whatever you bind on earth will be bound in heaven, and whatever you loose on earth will be loosed in heaven"* (Matt. 16:19 NKJV).

God has divinely committed His authority to rule and reign on earth to believers in His Son, just as He intended with Adam and Eve before they fell into sin. There is nothing outside of your dominion if you walk in relationship with God through prayer. You have been restored by Jesus Christ to exercise the same authority on earth as the last Adam (Jesus) did while He walked the earth. Holding the keys of the Kingdom of Heaven gives you authority. He who has the key to a gate has authority over the gate and whatever it protects. Jesus was telling His disciples that He was giving them Heaven's authority to use it on earth, especially to rule over the devil and his demonic activities.

The prayer of authority is not like ordinary prayer, which flows from earth to Heaven. Ordinary prayers are prayers of praise, supplication, intercession, thanksgiving, and consecration. These are prayers that move from earth to Heaven. The prayer of authority flows from Heaven to earth, directing God's effects on earth. You must connect with Heaven before exercising your authority in prayer. The court of Heaven must bind what you want to be bound on earth and loose what you want loosed.

People with the spirit of prayer have the highest interest in the courts of Heaven, where authority is released to them as they pray. When they engage in spiritual warfare, they don't even have to say, "I take authority" over that situation or the devil. Those who already have authority in Christ simply have to exercise it. The Church has been given this authority to rule over demons and everything satan controls. Jesus reaffirmed this in a later discussion with the disciples when He told them, *"Assuredly, I say to you, whatever you bind on earth will be bound in heaven, and whatever you loose on earth will be loosed in heaven"* (Matt. 18:18 NKJV).

Since Jesus is the head of the Church, your connection to Him gives you the ability to access God's power and authority. If you learn how to exercise your authority in prayer, you will see many problems in life resolved. The only way you can exercise dominion and control is through the prayer of authority. This is the most crucial, spiritual prayer in the Bible because it commands God to carry out His purpose and words on the earth. *"Thus says the Lord, the Holy One of Israel, and his Maker: 'Ask Me of things to come concerning My sons; and concerning the work of My hands, you command Me'"* (Isa. 45:11 NKJV).

In this verse, God is telling His children that—through prayer—they can make requests of Him in connection with the work of His hands. This demonstrates the results of the prayer of authority: Heaven rules on the earth. What an awesome responsibility that leaves in your hands and mine. It is up to believers on the earth to exercise heavenly authority in order to bring everything contrary to God's plan under the obedience of Christ. Stop talking to God about your obstacles and tell the mountain about your God. Remind it of Christ's promise in Mark:

> *For assuredly, I say to you, whoever says to this mountain, "Be removed and be cast into the sea," and does not doubt in his heart, but believes that those things he says will be done, he will have whatever he says* (Mark 11:23 NKJV).

This passage from Mark is talking about the prayer of authority. Jesus begins it by saying in verse 22, *"Have faith in God."* All authority a believer exercises comes from Heaven. Notice in verse 23 that Jesus didn't say to talk to God about the mountain or look at it or shout at it. He said to command the mountain and tell it where to go. This mountain could be sickness or anything contrary to God's plans or purposes for your life.

Praying with this kind of authority will help you be an overcomer—one who does what Jesus did while He was on the earth. An overcomer knows how to bring God's kingdom down to earth through prayer. An overcomer recognizes that he (or she) is seated with Jesus in the heavenly places and releases faith from that position to accomplish something on earth. Prayer is the only way to activate God's power to overcome the devil and his work. *Only those who pray the prayer of authority become overcomers in life.* They know the truth of these Scriptures:

> *For whatever is born of God overcomes the world. And this is the victory that has overcome the world; our faith. Who is he who overcomes the world, but he who believes that Jesus is the Son of God?* (1 John 5:4-5 NKJV)

And they overcame him by the blood of the Lamb and by the word of their testimony, and they did not love their lives to the death (Revelation 12:11 NKJV).

Under Authority

You can't exercise God's authority in your life if you are not under God's authority. I have seen many believers unable to exercise God's authority because they are not subject to God's authority over their lives. As James 4:7 says, *"Therefore submit to God. Resist the devil and he will flee from you"* (NKJV).

Remember that God has entrusted His authority to rule over earth to you. It is your deep-rooted understanding of this authority, how it works, when to use it, and your relationship with Christ that makes you effective in the demonstration of God's authority in prayer. Before you pray the prayer of authority, you must know what is bound in Heaven and what is loosed in Heaven. Then order God to fulfill His will.

Pray this prayer:

Heavenly Father, I recognize this day that as You have sent Jesus into the world, even so Jesus has sent me into this world to exercise the same heavenly authority over prevailing circumstances on earth. Holy Spirit, empower my prayer life to be always in harmony with heavenly decrees so I can effectively demonstrate God's authority on earth. In Jesus' name, amen.

Endnote

1. David O. Oyedepo, *Winning Prayer* (Ogen State, Nigeria: Dominion Publishing House, 2009).

CHAPTER EIGHT

The Wonders of God's Will

Prayer is the pathway to finding God's will.

With Kuwait officially embracing the Islamic faith and 85 percent of the population reported to be Muslims,[1] you might not expect this nation to be the scene of a prayer that determined a life-changing course for one of Christ's followers. Yet, this is exactly what happened during my month-long visit to the Middle East in May of 2009. A young man who works for an investment company there came to see me, seeking direction for a key decision he had to make.

He held a good job and had been with the company for several years. In fact, he attributed finding this position to prayer. Still, Kuwait didn't offer him the most conducive environment for raising a family because of his problems with the educational system and some other, personal factors. Two years before, he had moved them to the United States, but didn't find a good job. His company agreed to rehire him, and he left his family in the States, flying back every few months to visit them. Now he was contemplating whether to resign so he could join his family or remain in his position, which provided enough income to support him and a family overseas. He desperately wanted to know God's will. Despite his loneliness, he was prepared to do whatever the Lord wanted, including staying put.

"Lord, I pray this man will be able to find the pathway to Your will for his life," I began. As we continued in prayer, I sensed a definite impression from God: it was His will that this man remain in Kuwait for another 7 to 12 months. In that window of time, he would be able to accomplish some needed tasks for his employer. After that, God would make it evident when he should leave and rejoin his family. As soon as I relayed this message, his face lit up. It turned out this message confirmed what his wife had already told him.

"Pastor, can I tell you the truth?" he said, smiling. "This is God's will for me. Two months ago, my wife had been asking the Lord, 'Why did You allow this? Why do we have to be separated? When will my husband be able to join us?' God assured her that I would be able to join the family by September of 2010. Your telling me to stay for a while longer was a confirmation of what she had already told me."

It is truly a wonder when you discover God's will in prayer since the safest place you can ever be is in the center of His will. The wonder of following God's will brings rest and satisfaction to the one who carries it out. Uncovered through prayer, this satisfaction can be compared to a baby resting in the arms of her mother while her mother moves throughout her day. There is nothing on earth that can overcome a believer who consistently walks in God's will. This kind of obedience guarantees a life of extraordinary success and fulfillment.

There are three areas I will focus on in this chapter.

1. What is the will of God?

2. How does prayer help you find the will of God?

3. How do you prepare yourself to find the will of God?

What Is the Will of God?

In John 4:34, Jesus said, *"My food is to do what the One who sent Me wants Me to do and to finish His work."* From this verse we can define the will of God as the plans, desires, intents, and purposes that He wants to see fulfilled on the earth. God has something within His heart that He wants to come to pass, and He is waiting for humans to discover it through prayer. Because He chose to delegate the task, it is something men and women must do. This divine impression in God's heart is His will. We need to seek for it as Christ did. Jesus told His disciples that His food—meaning the substance that sustained Him—was to carry out His Father's plans.

King David was a great man who discovered God's agenda because of his commitment to a lifestyle of prayer. More than half of the book of Psalms consist of his prayers. David earnestly sought to know God's agenda, and because of his devotion to knowing His will, he became known for his closeness to God despite his mistakes:

> *And when He had removed him, He raised up for them David as king, to whom also He gave testimony and said, "I have found David the son of Jesse, a man after My own heart, who will do all My will"* (Acts 13:22 NKJV).

On the other hand, satan does not want God's will to be done. He does not want people to find it or follow it. The devil attacks people who want to do God's will by bringing distractions, confusion, fleshly lusts, or pride to their souls. He tried to distract Jesus from doing His Father's will by tempting Jesus. Satan showed Him all the kingdoms of the world and promised to give it all to Christ if only He would worship him. This was a blatant attempt to stop Jesus from fulfilling God's will of dying on the cross for mankind. The devil offered Jesus a way out by trying to deceive Him into accepting glory without the cross.

Since Jesus came to earth to fulfill His Father's purpose, He refused the bait. Throughout His earthly ministry, Jesus committed Himself to this heavenly aim. Like David, Jesus fulfilled the will of God on earth: *"The devil has been sinning since the beginning, so anyone who continues to sin belongs to the devil. The Son of God came for this purpose: to destroy the devil's work"* (1 John 3:8).

The apostle Paul was another great man who discovered God's will for his life and committed himself to fulfilling it. Consumed with passion to follow God, not even the threat of death turned him aside from this pursuit. Paul's obsession for the will of God kept him from being distracted by satanic forces. At the end of his ministry, he wrote, *"My life is being given as an offering to God, and the time has come for me to leave this life. I have fought the good fight, I have finished the race, I have kept the faith"* (2 Tim. 4:6-7).

Every believer has a course to follow—finding the will of God. You must make up your mind to strive in prayer and never to settle for anything outside His will since that is what brings Him ultimate glory. This is what Paul sought, not only for himself, but also for fellow believers. When he wrote to the church at Colosse, he promised to pray continually for them to be filled with this knowledge:

> *Because of this, since the day we heard about you, we have continued praying for you, asking God that you will know fully what He wants. We pray that you will also have great wisdom and understanding*

in spiritual things so that you will live the kind of
life that honors and pleases the Lord in every way
(Colossians 1:9-10).

Any time you find the will of God through prayer, you will experience God's burden. A deep yearning to see His will fulfilled will come upon you, driving you into the labor room of prayer. There the spirit of prayer and intercession will overtake you.

Finding God's Will

Prayer is the pathway to finding God's plans. Every one who discovers and fulfills God's purposes discovers them through the channel of prayer. As we fellowship with God, we come to know what He wants. When we do, we have to be careful to listen. The prophet Jeremiah warned his fellow Israelites,

> *This is what the Lord says, "Stand where the roads*
> *cross and look. Ask where the old way is, where the*
> *good way is, and walk on it. If you do, you will find*
> *rest for yourselves. But they have said, 'We will not*
> *walk on the good way'"* (Jeremiah 6:16).

God has plans within His heart that are like a well-worn path, something He wants to reveal so you can carry it out. Yet He requires you to ask in prayer. Until you ask the Lord about the good way and listen for His answer, you can never walk on the path. Until you discover God's will, you will follow your own will. The one who prays not only approaches God often, but will frequently find and follow His will.

Prayer is communication between God and people. As you fellowship with God in prayer, you submit your will and thoughts to Him. Then His will and thoughts can be reproduced in you. In teaching His disciples about prayer, Jesus shows an example of how prayer creates the avenue for God's will to be reproduced: *"After this manner therefore pray ye: Our Father which art in heaven, hallowed be Thy name. Thy kingdom come. Thy will be done in earth, as it is in heaven"* (Matt. 6:9-10 KJV). Through this passage, Christ gives us a pattern by which we can approach God in prayer so He can reproduce His will in us.

Through the Lord's Prayer, Jesus teaches several lessons:

- We must start with a personal relationship with God and other believers *("Our Father")*. Our prayers must possess faith. *"Which art in heaven"* means that even though we don't see God, we have faith that He lives in Heaven.

- Our prayers must include worship, as expressed in the phrase, *"Hallowed be Thy name."*

- We must come to God with expectations, particularly the anticipation that His Kingdom will come on this earth.

- We must submit to God. *"Thy will be done on earth, as it is in heaven"* is the place where our thoughts and will enter God's thoughts.

God has plans He wants to see fulfilled on earth, but He is looking for human vessels who are eager to follow them. This kind of obedience results from prayer. Those who pray earnestly can feel what God feels, think what God thinks, and see what God sees. They can imitate Christ in the Garden of Gethsemane:

> *Then Jesus went about a stone's throw away from them. He kneeled down and prayed, "Father, if You are willing, take away this cup of suffering. But do what You want, not what I want"* (Luke 22:41-42).

The Bible teaches that even when we come to a crossroads in life, if we give ourselves to fervent prayer, our will (which is usually difficult to let go of) comes under submission to God's. Just as Jesus submitted to His Father, you can submit your will and thoughts to God. Prayer is where we surrender our minds, emotions, thoughts, and wills to God. Once you pray and discover His will, you can bring glory to Him: *"Now this is the confidence that we have in Him, that if we ask anything according to His will, He hears us"* (1 John 5:14 NKJV).

Praying according to the will of God is the most effective and spiritual prayer. Every believer must learn to pray this way, but you can't if you don't know the Father's will for every situation. Jesus stayed in touch with His Father constantly during His earthly ministry. Because He spent time alone with Him in prayer, He stayed in His will. And because He prayed in accordance with God's wishes, Jesus never experienced unanswered prayer. It is impossible to find and do the will of God without a commitment to prayer. As Psalm 16:11 says, *"You will show me the path of life; in Your presence is fullness of joy; at Your right hand are pleasures forevermore"* (NKJV).

God is willing to show us His path of life, but only when we go into our prayer closets. In His presence, God makes His plans known to those who seek Him with a committed heart. When your pursuit of God mingles with denial of self, the outcome leads you to His will. The person committed to pursue God with sincere desire and a willingness to surrender to Him is the one God can trust with His will.

Self poses the greatest obstacle to this search; once you decide to die to self interest, you become a vessel ready to fulfill God's will on the earth. You can't be full of self-centered ways and ask God to reveal His plans. His will comes with a price. You must possess the same desire as David when he wrote,

God, You are my God. I search for You. I thirst for
You like someone in a dry, empty land where there is
no water. I have seen You in the Temple and have seen
Your strength and glory....I stay close to You; You
support me with Your right hand (Psalm 63:1-2,8).

Committed to seeking God, David gave himself to the pursuit of prayer without yielding to any distractions. Because of his commitment, the Lord regularly revealed to him His will and other insights, even Christ on the cross (see Ps. 22:1). David became a vessel through which God's plans and purposes were fulfilled in his day.

Learn From David

The opposition David faced after the Amalekites raided Ziklag offers excellent instruction on how the prayer of inquiry can help you find and do the will of God, even in difficult and stressful circumstances. First, the story:

On the third day, when David and his men arrived
at Ziklag, he found that the Amalekites had raided
southern Judah and Ziklag, attacking Ziklag and
burning it. They captured the women and everyone,
young and old, but they had not killed anyone. They
had only taken them away. When David and his men
came to Ziklag, they found the town had been burned
and their wives, sons, and daughters had been taken
as prisoners. Then David and his army cried loudly
until they were too weak to cry anymore.

David's two wives had also been taken—Ahinoam
of Jezreel and Abigail the widow of Nabal from
Carmel. The men in the army were threatening
to kill David with stones, which greatly upset
David. Each man was sad and angry because his
sons and daughters had been captured, but David

> *found strength in the Lord his God. David said to*
> *Abiathar the priest, "Bring me the holy vest." Then*
> *David asked the Lord, "Should I chase the people*
> *who took our families? Will I catch them?" The Lord*
> *answered, "Chase them. You will catch them, and*
> *you will succeed in saving your families"* (1 Samuel
> 30:1-8).

Even though he had to endure complaints from his followers, David didn't quickly set out on the path of revenge. He first asked God what he should do. When you voice the prayer of inquiry, God will show you what you need to do in order to get what you are looking for—which will bring glory to Him. Numerous believers want God to reveal His will to them about their situation or life, but are unwilling to take responsibility and put to work what God has revealed to them from His written Word. For example, believers who are in financial distress are often unwilling to obey God's directive to give sacrificially to His Kingdom. God will not reveal His will to you in a way that contradicts His Word.

There are three things you need to learn from this situation and how David overcame it:

1. YOU MUST ENCOURAGE YOURSELF IN THE LORD. The first thing David did was make sure the Lord would take care of his soul. Discouragement affects your mind, will, and emotions. Only those who keep their minds free of discouragement and worry can engage in the prayer of inquiry to learn God's will. Fretting drains your boldness to go to Him in prayer and quenches the Spirit of God within you. That destroys your ability to freely communicate with Him. Hebrews teaches us to go before Him confidently:

> *Let us, then, feel very sure that we can come before*
> *God's throne where there is grace. There we can*

receive mercy and grace to help us when we need it
(Hebrews 4:16).

2. YOU MUST GO BEFORE GOD WITH A PURE HEART.
David asked for the holy vest (also known as an "ephod"),
which was a garment the priest wore around his chest—close
to his heart—before he entered God's presence. David did this
because he wanted God to take care of his spirit. Your heart
is your communication center with God (see Prov. 20:27).
When your mind and heart are mingled with the pure water of
holiness, then you are ready to engage in the prayer of inquiry.
Again, Hebrews teaches the necessity of a pure heart: *"Let us
come near to God with a sincere heart and a sure faith, because we
have been made free from a guilty conscience, and our bodies have
been washed with pure water"* (Heb. 10:22). A heart stained by
a guilty conscience can't receive God's will.

**3. YOU MUST ASK GOD FOR PLANS AND BE DETERMINED
TO CARRY THEM OUT.** The believer who prays, "Lord, what
must I do?" is mature and prepared to know God's ways.
Immature Christians say, "Oh, Lord, come and do it for me."
You must be like David, who inquired of God. Because he was
a man of inquiries, he never suffered defeats or injuries as a
warrior. He had access to divine instructions through his prayer,
which made a world of difference. Discovering God's will can
help keep you from a lifetime of struggles. God is waiting for
you to draw close to Him in prayer so He can reveal His plans
to you. James advises: *"Draw near to God and He will draw
near to you..."* (James 4:8 NKJV). If David had not drawn near
to God with his inquiries, God wouldn't have drawn near to
him with instructions on how to recover what his enemies had
stolen (see 1 Sam. 30:18-19).

Many voice prayers of petition, calling on God to intervene
and do something about their situation. But they often ignore
the place of inquiry, which will give them access to God's ways.

As long as you remain a spiritual babe, crying in the face of every tough circumstance, you will never manifest as a child of God. You will never be the powerful revelation the world is aching to see: *"For the earnest expectation of the creation eagerly waits for the revealing of the sons of God"* (Rom. 8:19 NKJV).

Maybe you are reading this book and have reached a crossroads. You see much confusion around you, and the joy of living has escaped from your heart. Maybe you feel unhappy with your occupation or station in life. You feel unfulfilled and outside the will of God for your life. I encourage you to get into God's presence. Ask Him to show you what steps you need to take. Make up your mind to not leave until He reveals His will. Determine to place Him above any circumstances and trust Him to do as the prophet Jeremiah promised:

> *"I say this because I know what I am planning for you," says the Lord. "I have good plans for you, not plans to hurt you. I will give you hope and a good future. Then you will call My name. You will come to Me and pray to Me, and I will listen to you. You will search for Me. And when you search for Me with all your heart, you will find Me"* (Jeremiah 29:11-13).

Though prayer is where you will discover the thoughts of God's heart toward you, it will require a calm, restful, undivided heart to discover what God wants to do in your life. If you are serious about finding God's will, you must make the prayer of inquiry a lifestyle, something you do for the rest of your life. The story of Jesus praying before choosing His disciples (see Luke 6:12-13) is a vivid example of how we can only find God's will through prayer. Christ did not choose 12 disciples without first bathing the decision in an all-night prayer session. That enabled Him to know who to choose.

This should be the pattern of every Christian leader who wants to do the will of God and bring glory to Him. Too many people in ministry today are carrying out tasks outside of God's will. They occupy positions they weren't appointed to, nor were they anointed by God to occupy them. These ministers may have gifts, but no anointing for the office because God only anoints those he appoints but people's appointments carries no anointing. And God only anoints you when you are at the center of His will. If Jesus spent all night praying to find God's mind, you should be equally serious about any decision you make. Never make a decision without first cooking it in prayer.

Preparing to Find God's Will

If you want to seek God's will for your life, you must take preparation seriously. Most people prepare when they have to take an exam or other tests, but when it comes to asking God about the blueprint of their lives, they take it for granted. Only those who prepare their ways before the Lord will find greatness. God will not speak to you if you don't create the atmosphere for Him to reveal His will.

As you listen for His voice, remember that it will be peaceful: *"I will listen to God the Lord. He has ordered peace for those who worship Him. Don't let them go back to foolishness"* (Ps. 85:8). A heart lacking peace will never hear God's voice or know His will because it is full of distractions and is not focused on God. If you want to know God's will in prayer, you have to de-program your mind of everything that you are going through. Cleanse the channels of your mind and heart from the world's cares. Put your mind and spirit in a position where they are worry-free.

I personally encourage believers to engage in prayers of inquiry mostly around midnight, which is the most peaceful and quiet hour. Jesus used the night to seek His Father's mind (see Luke 6:12-13). David was another diligent seeker who also sought God in the night (see Ps. 16:7; 19:2). God commits Himself to reveal His will to you when He has your undivided attention. So many believers go to God in prayer in order to know God's will, but their hearts are full of distractions. They don't give Him quality time. They would rather listen to the news or watch television than spend time with God. In such a state, they can't hear God or know His will.

Let me close this chapter by outlining three steps that can prepare you to hear God and know His will:

1. Take Christ's authority to silence the enemy while you pray.

2. Ask the Lord to clear any presumptions and preconceived ideas from your mind.

3. Wait and believe He will speak in the way and the time that He chooses. Don't be in a hurry to stop waiting.

Pray this prayer:

Lord, I surrender to Your will. Teach me to always seek Your mind in every situation that I face. May I not waste precious time wandering when I can come directly to You and seek direction for my life. In Jesus' name, amen.

Endnote

1. http://www.cia.gov/library/publications/the-world-factbook/geos/ku.html.

CHAPTER NINE

The Wonders of Heaven on Earth

*Prayer enforces the Kingdom and will of
God on earth.*

Millions flock to Florida's beaches for sun, fun, and relaxation, but when I traveled to Cocoa Beach in September of 2004, I experienced a much bigger thrill than riding an ocean wave. It happened in the branch office of a national bank and financial service center. As I waited on a business appointment, I saw a young man walk into the lobby to make a deposit. As I gazed at him, I noticed he was wearing hearing aids in both ears. Suddenly, the Holy Spirit told me to ask him why he was wearing them. When I did, he replied, "Because I can barely hear without them. I'm almost totally deaf."

"Do you believe in God?" I asked.

"Yes, I believe in Jesus Christ. I'm a Christian."

"Do you believe God can heal you?" I pressed.

"Well, I believe," he said, then hesitated. "But I also believe my hearing problem is part of my suffering for Christ."

"Where did you get that doctrine?" I asked, proceeding to explain that deafness and other sicknesses are not part of God's plan for our lives. Jesus called the devil a thief who comes to steal, kill, and destroy (see John 10:10), I said, and satan delights in persuading people that his damaging work somehow fulfills God's will. What God wanted to do was heal him, not see him fight this infirmity, I added. After a few more minutes of conversation, he asked if I would pray for him.

"Do you think God can heal you?" I asked.

"Yes," he said, nodding.

Removing the hearing aids from his ears, I laid both hands on his ears and asked God to heal him and manifest His power in this man's body. When I finished praying, I removed my hands from his ears and whispered in his ears to see if he could hear me.

"I can hear the sounds of people walking into the bank!" he exclaimed. "When you prayed for me, I could hear my ears pop open. This is wonderful!"

Establishing Wonders

This story shows how prayer establishes the wonders of Heaven on earth. Heaven is the Father and the earth is the mother, the soil where Heaven's seed can grow. The earth produces its fruits when Heaven releases its rain. God's greatest desire is to see His Kingdom come to earth as it is in Heaven. Before going further, I want to review definitions of the Kingdom and will of God:

- The Kingdom of God is simply defined as the dominion of a King. God rules Heaven and controls everything that happens there, just as everything that takes place on earth is under the control of the King of Heaven.

- As you read in the last chapter, the will of God is His plans, ways, desires, and thoughts. Just as humans have a mind that involves the will, thoughts, and emotions, so does God.

God, the King of Heaven, created the earth and gave it to humanity as our kingdom: *"The heaven, even the heavens, are the Lord's; but the earth He has given to the children of men"* (Ps. 115:16 NKJV). God's original plan during creation was for humanity—whom He created in His image (see Gen. 1:26)— to rule the earth as God would rule it. God's creative intent for making men and women in His image was for them to be an extension of His heavenly Kingdom on earth. But when they followed satan's instructions and sin entered the world, they lost this divine capacity. Sin destroyed God's creative mind and life in Adam and Eve's souls (see Gen. 2:7). This tragedy meant they could no longer function as kings.

After reviewing the situation, God decided to revisit His original plan of extending Heaven's Kingdom. He accomplished that plan by sending His Son, Jesus, to perfect the work that Adam failed to complete. Jesus came to restore humans to God's image and His plan to rule and reign. Jesus was the seed of God placed in Mary's womb (see Luke 1:31-35), which the Father did to give His Son two natures. As the Son of man, He carried an earthly nature; as the Son of God, He carried a heavenly nature, just like the first Adam. Though I don't plan to delve deeper into this topic, I encourage you to study some books that explore this great mystery.[1]

Jesus is the heavenly Man who came with the mission to establish God's Kingdom and bring Heaven's domain to earth. His earthly ministry demonstrated that. Everything He did on earth lined up with the heavenly Kingdom where His Father dwells. Christ fully expressed God in bodily form on earth:

> *...who being the brightness of His glory and the express image of His person, and upholding all things by the word of His power, when He had by Himself purged our sins, sat down at the right hand of the Majesty on high* (Hebrews 1:3 NKJV).

Christ accomplished this awesome mission through His death and resurrection.

Before He returned to Heaven to be with His Father, Jesus planted the seed of God's nature in His disciples. When the Holy Spirit came upon them, it gave life to this seed and birthed the Church. The Church became the extension of God's Kingdom.

> *No one can see God, but Jesus Christ is exactly like him. He ranks higher than everything that has been made....He is the head of the body, which is the church. Everything comes from Him. He is the first one who was raised from the dead. So in all things Jesus has first place* (Colossians 1:15,18).

Working out His Kingdom

Though Jesus is the Kingdom's heavenly Head, we are the earthly members. God's purpose is to work out His Kingdom and will on earth through His followers and their prayers. Without God we cannot work out His will. Without us, He will not manifest His Kingdom on earth. As Hebrews 11:40 says, *"God having provided something better for us, that they should not be made perfect apart from us"* (NKJV).

Without God's Kingdom and will, prayer is baseless. Without prayer, God's Kingdom and will lay dormant. Prayer makes them active and practical. When the Kingdom of God (His domain) comes, His will (or mind) is being done on the earth. Prayer puts God's will to practical uses, making it seed in a nourishing soil. What Christianity needs today above all else is men and women who can through prayer put God to the task of bringing down His throne and making His power known on earth. Our cry can be expressed as the prophet Isaiah's was years ago:

> *Tear open the skies and come down to earth so that the mountains will tremble before You. Like a fire that burns twigs, like a fire that makes water boil, let Your enemies know who You are. Then all nations will shake with fear when they see You. You have done amazing things we did not expect. You came down, and the mountains trembled before You* (Isaiah 64:1-3).

This passage teaches that when Heaven opens, God comes down to earth to reveal His presence. At the beginning of chapter 64, Isaiah was praying for the people of Israel, asking that the Heavens be opened so God's Kingdom could be made manifest to His people. Through his prayer, Isaiah shows the outcome of Heaven visiting the earth. Mountains, which refer to spiritual obstacles, move. Rivers of living water within the believer (see John 7:38) are fired to the boiling point so the Lord's name is revealed to God's enemies. When God visits the earth, nations tremble and miracles take place. Isaiah's prayer proves that God's Kingdom can only be manifested to people and in places where they invite Him. God will not go where He is not invited, which is why your prayers are crucial for the advancement of His Kingdom. *Prayer is the force that attracts the attention of God's domain and accomplishes His will on the earth.*

Through the person of Jesus, God and His will are planted as seeds in the hearts of believers. The Holy Spirit activates the Kingdom of God within us when we labor with Him in prayer. Christ taught that this Kingdom was within humans:

> *Some of the Pharisees asked Jesus, "When will the kingdom of God come?" Jesus answered, "God's kingdom is coming, but not in a way that you will be able to see with your eyes. People will not say, 'Look, here it is!' or, 'There it is!' because God's kingdom is within you"* (Luke 17:20-21).

Jesus was saying that God's domain, center, action, dwelling, and lifestyle are headquartered in you. This Kingdom is invisible, inactive, and motionless until the Spirit of God comes upon you through fervent prayer and enforces God's lifestyle, activating it for the blessing of people on the earth.

The practicality of God's Kingdom becomes a living reality through the force of prayer. Without it, you will never see the manifestation of God's Kingdom inside of you. In the days of the early Church, Christ's disciples recognized that when activated in them, God's realm made a world of difference in their ministry. This became evident when the devil attempted to stop God's activity in their lives through persecution and threats. These believers turned themselves over to God in earnest prayer, releasing the Spirit of God in fresh life and power. This helped them manifest the reality of God's Kingdom:

> *When the believers heard this, they prayed to God together, "Lord, You are the One who made the sky, the earth, the sea, and everything in them.... And now, Lord, listen to their threats. Lord, help us, Your servants, to speak Your word without fear. Show us Your power to heal. Give proofs and make miracles happen by the power of Jesus, Your holy*

servant." After they had prayed, the place where they were meeting was shaken. They were all filled with the Holy Spirit, and they spoke God's word without fear....With great power the apostles were telling people that the Lord Jesus was truly raised from the dead. And God blessed all the believers very much (Acts 4:24,29-31,33).

The Christian's Trade

Reformation leader Martin Luther once said, "The Christian's trade is praying." Whether a pastor, evangelist, accountant, attorney, banker, business owner, or assembly-line worker, a believer's other vocation should be prayer. Those who know nothing of this trade will never experience its benefits. If the early believers had not engaged in prayers linked to God's heart, they would have gone out of the business of bringing God's Kingdom to earth. Prayer enforces God's Kingdom and will on the earth.

Too many believers are waiting on God to manifest His Kingdom and will in their lives. I have heard such people say, "Well, we can't do anything about this situation unless God comes and does it for us." While they are waiting for God to act, God is waiting for them to engage Him in prayer so His Spirit can quicken His lifestyle in them in order to change the circumstances around them. The move of God in Heaven begins with the move of humans on earth.

God is waiting on you to come to Him in prayer with a broken spirit so He can send rain on your spiritual dryness. Psalm 34:18 says, *"The Lord is close to the brokenhearted, and He saves those whose spirits have been crushed,"* while Psalm 51:17 adds, *"The sacrifice God wants is a broken spirit...."* In Genesis 7:11-12, the Bible describes how the earth's underground springs split open before the windows of Heaven poured out the waters of the Great Flood. If the fountains deep within the earth refuse to break open, neither will the windows of Heaven follow. Earth is the place that provokes the move of Heaven. Prayer is an invitation to Heaven. When God's people turn to Him with a repentant heart, He sends His Spirit over the earth so His Kingdom and will are revealed. Solomon put it this way: *"Turn at my rebuke; surely I will pour out my spirit on you; I will make my words known to you"* (Prov. 1:23 NKJV).

Like electricity, God's Kingdom and will may sparkle and dazzle, yet remain impotent for good until these dynamic, life-giving currents are chained by the prayers of believers, causing the mighty forces of God's power to move and bless people. A believer can only carry the current of God's power through a commitment to prayer, which makes it possible for the wonders of Heaven to be seen on earth.

The Coming Kingdom

As Jesus was praying, one of His disciples asked Him to teach them how to pray:

> *Now it came to pass, as He was praying in a certain place, when He ceased, that one of His disciples said to Him, "Lord, teach us to pray, as John also taught his disciples." So He said to them, "When you pray, say: Our Father in heaven, hallowed be Your name. Your kingdom come. Your will be done on earth as it is in heaven"* (Luke 11:1-2 NKJV).

Note that the disciples didn't ask Jesus to teach them how to love people, win the world, or preach, but how to pray. Why is prayer so important? Why did Christ give it so much attention? It's because prayer is what knits Heaven and earth together. Without prayers on earth, Heaven has no channel to flow the resources and blessings that God created to earth.

Jesus taught His disciples to pray with sincere concern for the Kingdom and will of God to be done on earth. This Kingdom-oriented praying gives you open access to God. The opening of the Lord's Prayer focuses on meeting God's needs. *"Our Father"* concerns your relationship with God and other believers; *"in heaven"* deals with your faith connection to God. *"Hallowed be Your name"* pertains to your worship of God. All these points address God's greatest need: the coming of His Kingdom and His will being accomplished on earth. Only through prayer can you meet this need. And God's need comes before anything we so commonly worry about. In the Sermon on the Mount, Jesus told the crowds not to worry about food, clothing, and other necessities: *"But seek first the kingdom of God and His righteousness, and all these things shall be added to you"* (Matt. 6:33 NKJV).

If you want to live a life of divine fulfillment and operate under an open Heaven, the best way is to program yourself to meet the needs of God in your prayer life. Once you commit yourself to this, God will commit to meeting your needs, even before you ask. Look again at Isaiah, who wrote, *"I will provide for their needs before they ask, and I will help them while they are still asking for help"* (Isa. 65:24). This promise can only be enjoyed by those who commit to a Kingdom-based lifestyle of prayer. If you focus on seeking the Kingdom of God and possess a strong desire to see His will accomplished, you will become a vessel for God's blessings.

Two Kinds of Prayer

There are two primary kinds of prayer, one that meets the needs of God (see Luke 11:2) and the kind that meets the needs of people (see Luke 11:3-4). Both get God's attention. "Prayer of the Kingdom" brings glory to God and reveals His Kingdom and power on earth. When your prayers are centered on "me, myself, and I," you are asking God to meet your needs while His needs go unfulfilled. God's realm is not fully revealed and active today because the believers God wants to use don't engage in meeting His needs in prayer. Will you answer this call? Will you decide to pray less about your own desires and more about God's needs? Will you allow the Holy Spirit to give you a burden for the prayer of the Kingdom?

As you read, I trust the Holy Spirit—the ultimate author of this book—will give you the grace to labor in prayer. The wonders of Heaven are waiting for your prayers so they can manifest on the earth. As Christ said, *"Let your light so shine before men, that they may see your good works and glorify your Father in heaven"* (Matt. 5:16 NKJV). Just as Jesus is the light of this world (see John 9:5), you are the light of Jesus in the world. Your connection to Him through the prayer of the Kingdom will cause His light to shine before people. This brings glory to God in Heaven.

Acts describes Barnabas and Paul as men who gave their lives to serve the Lord Jesus. Through their undivided commitment to God's cause, they invaded Lystra with the Gospel of God's Kingdom. They demonstrated the lifestyle of His Kingdom to the people in this region. As Heaven came to earth, God's glory became apparent to everyone:

> *And they were preaching the gospel there. And in Lystra a certain man without strength in his feet was sitting, a cripple from his mother's womb, who had never walked. This man heard Paul speaking. Paul, observing him intently and seeing that he had faith to be healed, said with a loud voice, "Stand up straight on your feet!" And he leaped and walked. Now when the people saw what Paul had done, they raised their voices, saying in the Lycaonian language, "The gods have come down to us in the likeness of men"* (Acts 14:7-11 NKJV).

Paul and Barnabas didn't accept this worship; the Bible notes:

> *"they tore their clothes and ran in among the multitude, crying out and saying, 'Men, why are you doing these things? We also are men with the same nature as you, and preach to you that you should turn from these useless things to the living God, who made the heaven, the earth, the sea, and all things that are in them, who in bygone generations allowed all nations to walk in their own ways."* (Acts 14:14-16 NKJV).

Despite their misguided enthusiasm, when the people of Lycaonia saw a cripple walk for the first time in his life, they could see that God had come to earth. Because of their fervent prayer lives, Paul and Barnabas were able to call on God's power. In reviewing the miracle that occurred in Lystra, it is important to note what took place before these two apostles arrived there:

> *Now in the church that was at Antioch there were certain prophets and teachers: Barnabas, Simeon who was called Niger, Lucius of Cyrene, Manaen who had been brought up with Herod the tetrarch, and Saul. As they ministered to the Lord and fasted, the Holy Spirit said, "Now separate to Me Barnabas and Saul for the work to which I have called them." Then, having fasted and prayed, and laid hands on them, they sent them away* (Acts 13:1-3 NKJV).

Through prayer the Kingdom of God came down and His will took place in Lystra—all because citizens of the Kingdom came to town. This is God's intent for you and me. Yet God's cause often remains quiet and motionless because of a lack of prayer. Prayer makes the will of God rich and fruitful, enabling His Kingdom to become a reality. God wants His people to produce His fruit by enforcing His will. This is why Jesus taught,

> *If you remain in Me and follow My teachings, you can ask anything you want, and it will be given to you. You should produce much fruit and show that you are My followers, which brings glory to My Father* (John 15:7-8).

When men and women of prayer discover God's will and through earnest, concentrated prayer enforce it on the earth, the reality of God's Word becomes evident in our world. This generation is looking for a living reality. They need substance, not empty, formal, lifeless religion. A vibrant faith that sets people free and focuses their attentions on serving God and loving others shows how Heaven is pregnant with an agenda for earth. Though people can discover this heavenly agenda through prayer, it also takes prayer to enforce this agenda. Just before He ascended to Heaven, Jesus told His disciples

> *to wait for the Promise of the Father, "which,"* He said, *"you have heard from Me; for John truly baptized with water, but you shall be baptized with the Holy Spirit not many days from now"* (Acts 1:4-5 NKJV).

Acts 2 describes how, after ten days of waiting in earnest prayer, the disciples received this very gift. Yet only those who waited expectantly in prayer experienced this promise. In Acts 3 they demonstrated the power of the Kingdom of God within them. This Kingdom has golden fruit, waiting to be plucked by the hand of prayer. Prayer not only receives this fruit, it ensures it is a blessing to humanity by making it a practical reality on the earth. Answers to your prayers are a public witness to the fulfillment of God's will.

The miracle described in Acts 3, of a lame man walking and Peter's powerful message to the Israelites, showed the world that the Kingdom of God had come to earth.

Israel Reclaimed

The story of Elijah in First Kings 18—which I mentioned briefly in the first two chapters—is a fascinating account that shows how the will of God inspires and energizes prayer. God directed Elijah to appear before King Ahab, promising to then send rain upon the earth. Before that time, it had not rained for about three years. Elijah obeyed these instructions and gathered all Israel and the prophets of Baal on Mount Carmel. There Elijah proved to the nation that the Lord who answered prayer with fire is the one true God. When they saw this miracle, the people turned their hearts back to Him, and Elijah slew 400 false prophets of Baal. Yet even after these demonstrations of God's power, the promise of rain still waited for Elijah's prayer. When he prayed earnestly, the Heavens opened.

Prayer takes hold of God's will, removes obstacles, and creates a highway for His glory to come to earth. Without prayer, the devil's supernatural forces will become an obstacle for the fulfillment of God's will. Prayer is like pipes that will transmit, preserve, and direct the rain of Heaven to fertilize and refresh mankind. The Kingdom of God manifested itself in Israel after Elijah's relentless prayer. This is the kind of faith we need to see in action today. The Kingdom and will of God is poorly executed on earth because believers fail to rest their faith on His Word and pray expectantly, believing that God will answer. Turn your faith upward and pray, believing God's Kingdom can flow through you to earth.

Pray this prayer:

Dear Lord, forgive me for becoming an obstacle to the manifestation of Your Kingdom and will on earth. My prayerlessness has given satanic forces the opportunity to create roadblocks to the fulfillment of God's will. Today, I release myself to pray passionately. Use me as the pipe that transmits, preserves, and directs the rain of Heaven to fertilize and refresh mankind. In Jesus' name, amen.

Endnote

1. Watchman Nee, *The Spiritual Man* (New York: Christian Fellowship Publishers, 1977).

CHAPTER TEN

The Wonders of Godly Exercise

Prayer is the exercise room to build up your faith.

I didn't want to accept the message the Holy Spirit delivered one hot summer evening in 2008 as I prayed in my hotel room in Cebu City in the Philippines. I sensed God telling me that He wanted me to help break the spirit of poverty and greed in the lives of the pastors and others attending the "Revelation of God's Power" conference. God said He would break those spirits if people were willing to release their faith and sow sacrificial gifts into His Kingdom.

I hesitated. Right then, I didn't have the faith to carry out these instructions. I had seen the conditions affecting the people. Many were struggling just to survive. They wore threadbare clothes and had little to eat. There were pastors laboring under heavy debt and wondering how they could come up with their next rent payment. What kind of impression would I leave the next day if I spoke out what many might misconstrue as a harsh message? I wrestled with this question through the evening before drifting off to sleep.

At midnight, I awoke, God's instructions still ringing in my ears. Climbing out of bed, I started praying in the Spirit. On I went for five hours until the light of dawn peeked through the curtains of my hotel room. Though ordinarily I would have been overcome by fatigue, I felt refreshed. Faith rose in my spirit. I knew what I had to do: Speak the words God had given me the night before.

When I went downstairs for breakfast, I encountered a man from South Korea in the dining room. He smiled at me; I smiled back. He started to speak, but it soon became obvious he knew little English. After struggling to piece together a sentence, he reached into his pocket, pulled out some coins, and poured them into my hand, saying, "Take, take."

I looked down and quickly counted some quarters; there was about $4. Since I had never met this man, I was puzzled. Then his wife dug in her pocketbook and handed me more quarters. Then they gave me more cash, some of it Australian money and some from New Zealand. Though it took awhile to cross the language barriers, I learned these people had come to the island of Cebu on vacation. But why were these strangers giving me money?

When I returned to my hotel room, it dawned on me that God had just confirmed what He had told me earlier. He wanted me to tell the people at the conference that He is the God who gives His children power to get wealth (see Deut. 8:18), which He wants them to use to build His Kingdom. If they were willing to get out of their "take" mode and start giving, they would see Him do powerful things. Before I left for the convention hall, He also told me to take all the cash I had and exchange it for Filipino currency.

That day, when it came my turn to speak, I talked about activating the covenant of God's blessing. As I finished, I said, "I am calling out those who are willing to sow financial seed for the next six months into the Kingdom of God—not to give it to me or those running this conference, but to other ministers who are here. You may not have the money, but if you will step out in faith, God will give you the money. Come forward and I will anoint you with oil and pray for you."

What happened next shocked me. Instead of getting angry, as I had feared, people leaped out of their seats and cheered. As they flooded toward the front, I started handing out the money that I had received at breakfast. So many people came I ran out of cash. That didn't matter. Bystanders handed me more money so I could continue giving it away. Awhile later, I sensed the Holy Spirit telling me to give away my last $100. I extended my hand and quietly slipped it to a pastor next to me. He turned around and gave it to another pastor who had pledged to sow money into another ministry, even though he had no idea where he would get it.

Before I departed for the States the next day, I heard numerous testimonies about the spirit of generosity that had erupted (they would be followed by several emails after I returned). Pastors had been out giving away money to help other people, as if Acts 2 had come to life again: *"Now all who believed were together, and had all things in common, and sold their possessions and goods, and divided them among all, as anyone had need"* (Acts 2:44-45 NKJV).

This experience demonstrates how prayer is the exercise room to build up your faith. Even though I lacked the faith initially, that five-hour-long prayer session gave me the resolve to carry out God's instructions. He helped me to stop looking at circumstances and to focus on what He wanted me to do.

Faith-Filled Prayers

God has purposely limited Himself to not responding to prayers voiced without faith. Faith believes that it is God's will to answer prayer. Two biblical examples of the necessity of faith come from James 5:15, *"And the prayer of faith shall save the sick, and the Lord shall raise him up..."* (KJV), and Hebrews 11:6, *"Without faith no one can please God. Anyone who comes to God must believe that He is real and that He rewards those who truly want to find Him."*

Those who come to God must do so because they believe He will do what He says in His Word. Yet every circumstance and the world's growing influence in the 21st century will challenge your faith. Even during His day, Jesus asked the question, *"Nevertheless, when the Son of Man comes, will He really find faith on the earth?"* (Luke 18:8 NKJV).

This subject requires attention as we approach the end of time. Since it is a vital topic, we need to know: what is the essence of faith? Faith is what makes life fulfilling. Salvation, healing, and victory are impossible without faith. Everything in life is commanded by its force. Christianity is worthless without it. When you review great exploits of men and women in the Bible, you will discover that they were people of faith and prayer.

Faith is the principal determining factor of every believer's status. Your height in life is determined by your level of faith. This is why you must give faith ultimate priority. There are too many believers who pray for the sake of praying without attaching faith to their prayers, and they see little profit. That is no surprise since Hebrews repeatedly warns that faith is necessary to a Christian's life: *"The Good News was preached to us just as it was to them. But the teaching they heard did not help them, because they heard it but did not accept it with faith"* (Heb. 4:2).

If you are not experiencing answered prayer, you need to ask yourself if you have been praying in faith. It is the prayer of faith that produces results. James taught on this necessity when he wrote, *"But when you ask God, you must believe and not doubt. Anyone who doubts is like a wave in the sea, blown up and down by the wind"* (James 1:6).

If faith is a vital principle in commanding God's attention, then what is faith? Here are some of faith's scriptural attributes:

- It is a practical expression of confidence in God and in His word (see Heb. 10:35-36).

- Faith is an act motivated by the Word of God (see John 2:1-11).

- It is a weapon of war (see Eph. 6:16; 1 Tim. 6:12).

- It is a translating, transforming force (see 2 Cor. 3:17-18; Eph. 2:8-9; Heb. 11:5; Rom. 4:19-20).

- It is the victory (see 1 John 5:4; Heb. 11:33-34).

- It is a real substance (see Eph. 6:16; Heb. 11:1).

- It is the baseline of the foundation of Christianity (see 2 Pet. 1:5; Ps. 11:3; Mark 6:5-6).

- It is an absolute must (see Heb. 11:6; John 3:7).

If you want to make a difference in your prayer life, you must understand this powerful weapon. You must grasp why you can't live without it. Prayer can help build your up faith so you can experience fruit in your prayer life.

Two Kinds of Faith

1. The Gift of Faith

This kind of faith is a sovereign gift from God, which comes to you for a reason and for a limited season. It is the faith God gives you to accomplish an objective in a certain situation. This kind normally comes with a specific mission and can prompt an amazing miracle. But when the situation ends for which you needed it, that faith may not reside in you any longer. There are many Christians reliving a great miracle that may have happened 20 years ago. Yet their faith has not grown since! So many believers celebrate past victories, thinking it was their faith that gave them the victory. They don't realize it was God's sovereign faith working in them.

This gift comes to you when God speaks a specific word into your spirit. When you obey that word, a miracle follows because God will make sure the word He gave to you comes to pass. It comes when God brings you before a Red Sea situation, such as that faced by Moses and the children of Israel (see Exod. 14:1-31). God led them to the Red Sea, creating a situation while giving Moses the sovereign faith to triumph over it. Likewise, you may face some trials that seem impossible to overcome, which is where faith will act as the cornerstone of your existence. Through His word, Jesus gave His faith to Peter to walk on water. Peter failed only when he took his eyes off the Lord and focused on the threatening storm around him (see Matt. 14:25-31).

This is how the gift of faith operates. There are some spectacular examples of the gift of faith in the Bible, such as when Joshua commanded the sun and the moon to stand still (see Josh. 10:12-14) or when Elijah controlled the weather (see 1 Kings 17:1). Other examples include Paul silencing Elymas (see Acts 13:8-11) and Peter speaking God's judgment on Ananias and Sapphira (see Acts 5).

2. Developed Faith

Also known as general faith, all believers have this kind of faith—it came to them when they gave their life to Christ. *"For by grace you have been saved through faith, and that not of yourselves; it is the gift of God"* (Eph. 2:8 NKJV). This faith is a seed, planted in your heart at the time of your salvation. It grows in degrees, depending on your desire to exercise. It can develop from little faith to great faith (see Matt. 14:29-31; Luke 7:2-9). With developed faith, if you start out with 20-cent faith and it grows to 90-cent faith, you can deal with any situation that takes the more expensive kind. However, if you have only known a sudden gift of faith on a singular occasion and never grown your faith, your development might be stuck at the 20-cent level.

Developed faith will stay with you and work in any situation in which you find yourself. As long as the problem does not exceed your level of growth, you will triumph. But if—like the disciples in the following story from Matthew 17—you come against a problem bigger than the faith you have developed, you may experience defeat:

> *And when they had come to the multitude, a man came to Him, kneeling down to Him and saying, "Lord, have mercy on my son, for he is an epileptic and suffers severely; for he often falls into the fire and often into the water. So I brought him to Your disciples, but they could not cure him." Then Jesus answered and said, "O faithless and perverse generation, how long shall I be with you? How long shall I bear with you? Bring him here to Me."*

> *And Jesus rebuked the demon, and it came out of him; and the child was cured from that very hour. Then the disciples came to Jesus privately and said, "Why could we not cast it out?" So Jesus said to them, "Because of your unbelief; for assuredly, I say to you, if you have faith as a mustard seed, you will say to this mountain, 'Move from here to there,' and it will move; and nothing will be impossible for you.*

However, this kind does not go out except by prayer and fasting" (Matthew 17:14-21 NKJV).

This passage shows that the disciples were unable to produce results with their faith even though Jesus had given them the authority to cast out evil spirits and heal disease and sickness (see Matt. 10:1-8). They had the capability and had been sent out to do this kind of work, yet they failed. Jesus sharply reproved them for not doing it. Their failure brought shame and confusion on them and discounted their Lord and His cause.

Why didn't their faith cast the devil out of this boy? They had not been nurturing their faith by prayer and fasting. The disciples' failure to pray broke the ability of faith. Prayerlessness meant they lacked the energy of a strong, authoritative faith. Jesus told them casting out the powerful spirit they faced required prayer and fasting. Such disciplines take considerable effort (if it was easy, everyone would do it). Yet it leads to the glory of answered prayers, one of the most convincing, faith-creating forces.

Your faith grows a little stronger each time you see an answer to prayer. Christ's faith embraced strength and authority because He lived a lifestyle of prayer and fasting. Look at Matthew 17:1-3 and you will discover that Jesus cast out the demon right after His fresh encounter with Heaven, where He talked with Moses and Elijah. The mountaintop was one of His secret places—I call it Christ's exercise room of prayer. This was where Jesus constantly went to build up His faith by fellowshipping with the Father.

Prayer is the womb that develops your faith, the currency of Heaven. Jesus gave Himself to a lifestyle of prayer. The disciples' failure to cast out the demon is a lesson about the union of faith, prayer, and fasting, and how prayer plays a powerful role in keeping us connected to God. The Lord gives every believer a measure of faith so that we relate with Him and overcome situations that come against us. Still, it is your responsibility to develop this faith. If you don't water it in the soil of your heart through prayer, it will never grow. A victorious Christian life requires faith, which is necessary to be an overcomer.

Mustard Seed Faith

This parable of the mustard seed contains additional instruction. Jesus told the disciples that not only did they need to engage in prayer and fasting, but that they needed stronger faith. In verse 20, He told the disciples that they also failed because of unbelief—which is different than no belief. Their belief fell below the standard of faith required to do the job. Their small, undeveloped kind prevented them from casting out the demon. Their unbelief was not the same as disbelief, which is a negative force. If they had no belief, they wouldn't have attempted to cast out the devil in the first place. Since they had little faith, they needed to return to the exercise room of prayer to build it up.

After telling them that one of their problems was unbelief, Christ went on to explain how they could grow out of substandard faith. Jesus said that if they had faith as a grain of mustard seed, they could move mountains. Many have mistakenly interpreted this to mean with a smidgen of faith as tiny as a mustard seed people can accomplish impossible feats. This is not what Christ was trying to teach. If so, He would not have used the word "unbelief" as one reason they couldn't cast out the devil. Rather, the Lord wanted to teach His followers that faith that grows in the same way a grain of mustard seed develops into a mighty plant. Faith can mature into a powerful force that heals the sick, casts out demons, and produces signs and wonders (see Mark 16:17-20).

In Matthew 13:31-32, Jesus explained how a grain of mustard seed is the least of all seeds, but when it grows it develops into a plant greater than an herb, becoming a tree where birds can nest in its branches. Christ was not teaching that little faith can accomplish greater things, but that growing faith will accomplish bigger things when nurtured by prayer and fasting.

Spiritual Gymnasium

The gymnasium, usually referred to as "the gym," is common amid America's widespread problem of obesity. However, the gym is more than a place for overweight people. Anybody who wants to stay in shape and remain in good health often visits a gym or health club. Most people go to build up their physical muscles and burn off excess fat. There are good reasons for exercise; the Bible even encourages it. But there is another kind of exercise that requires you to get into the spiritual gymnasium. Such godly exercise is more profitable. As Paul told Timothy, *"Reject profane and old wives' fables, and exercise yourself toward godliness"* (1 Tim. 4:7 NKJV).

In the spiritual, prayer is one of a believer's major exercises, helping him or her build up faith muscles. Spiritual muscles will affect your movement with God. Just as you can't move in the natural without the help of your muscles, you can't move God to act on your behalf without spiritual strength. Earlier, I quoted Hebrews 11:6, which says, *"Without faith no one can please God...."* The phrase *"please Him"* can also mean "move God," because when someone is pleased they are moved. So you can restate the first part of this verse, *"Without faith it is impossible to move God."* With spiritual muscles developed by prayer, your faith can move God in the spiritual realm.

James taught this lesson: *"For as the body without the spirit is dead, so faith without works is dead also"* (James 2:26 NKJV).

The apostle was saying that if there is no exercise or working out involved in building your faith, it is dead. Faith takes action. If it is to stay alive, it needs a constant workout. You must give yourself to exercise. The more time you spend in the spiritual gymnasium, the more muscles you develop. Prayer waters the seeds of faith until it grows and becomes a plant blooming with fruit. Faith comes from hearing the Word of God (see Rom. 10:17), but faith works by acting on the Word of God (see James 2:20-22). Hearing God's Word, obeying it, and speaking it are all avenues for your faith to grow. Prayer nurtures the process of your faith coming alive.

The Widow's Pot of Oil

The Old Testament story of the prophet, Elisha, and the widow's overflowing pot of oil demonstrates the role of prayer in building up your faith to act on the Word of God:

> *The wife of a man from the groups of prophets said to Elisha, "Your servant, my husband, is dead. You know he honored the Lord. But now the man he owes money to is coming to take my two boys as his slaves!" Elisha answered, "How can I help you? Tell me, what do you have in your house?" The woman said, "I don't have anything there except a pot of oil." Then Elisha said, "Go and get empty jars from all your neighbors. Don't ask for just a few. Then go into your house and shut the door behind you and your sons. Pour oil into all the jars, and set the full ones aside."*
>
> *So she left Elisha and shut the door behind her and her sons. As they brought the jars to her, she poured out the oil. When the jars were all full, she said to her son, "Bring me another jar." But he said, "There are no more jars." Then the oil stopped flowing. She went*

> *and told Elisha. And the prophet said to her, "Go,*
> *sell the oil and pay what you owe. You and your sons*
> *can live on what is left"* (2 Kings 4:1-7).

There were three instructions that Elisha gave to this woman so she would experience a breakthrough:

1. Borrow empty vessels from her neighbors. He wanted her to do everything possible to prepare for God's blessing.

2. Shut the door upon herself and her sons. Elisha didn't want her to become a public spectacle, but to quietly wait on God.

3. Pour out the oil from her vessel into the borrowed, empty ones.

When she carried out these instructions, a miracle took place. From this amazing and inspiring story, I want to focus on the second instruction to shut the door on herself and her sons. This closing of the door symbolizes the prayer closet. Elisha wasn't referring to a physical door as much as a spiritual one. Prayer is a communal act when churches or small groups gather, but much of the time it is a solitary, sacred moment of talking to your Father one-on-one.

This woman and her two sons entered into prayer to meditate on the word Elisha had given them. After prayer, faith came alive to act on the word and follow the third instruction to pour the oil into empty vessels. Because faith came alive, acting on the instruction came easy. Prayer becomes like the believer's spiritual kitchen, where you cook the Word of God and produce faith. Faith comes alive in you only when the Holy Spirit empties you of doubt and fills you with a knowing that it is impossible to fail. Only in a place of prayer can the Holy Spirit empty you of doubt. For this reason believers must learn to pray often in the Spirit; it will help clear their minds and give them the ability to exercise faith.

Praying in the Spirit

Praying in the Spirit is a God-ordained program for your benefit, the most effective way God designed for building up your faith. *"But dear friends, use your most holy faith to build yourselves up, praying in the Holy Spirit"* (Jude 1:20).

How does praying in the Spirit build up your faith? First, you must understand that faith is a spiritual force inside you. It is of the spirit, not a mental capability. Likewise, God is a Spirit (see John 4:24). Faith comes from God's Word to you. When you pray in the Spirit, your spirit communicates directly with God's Spirit, a spirit-to-spirit communication. In this form of prayer, your faith interacts with God and receives new strength:

> *Those who have the gift of speaking in different languages are not speaking to people; they are speaking to God. No one understands them; they are speaking secret things through the Spirit* (1 Corinthians 14:2).

As you pray in the Spirit, your spirit links up with God's Spirit and the Holy Spirit begins to purify the Word in your heart. The word of faith in your heart begins to form images, like moving pictures that you can see in your mind's eye. As you see the fulfillment of the Word, the Holy Spirit empties you of doubt and fills you with faith. In First Corinthians 14:4, Paul says that he who speaks in an unknown tongue edifies himself. We derive the word *edifice,* or "building," from the word, *edify.* When you pray in the Spirit or speak in tongues, the words may be a mystery to your human intellect, but you are building yourself up spiritually.

As you exercise yourself in praying in the Spirit, your faith grows a little stronger each time. Developing life in the Spirit is a walk of faith. Praying in tongues helps your faith grow because it is an act of faith. God gives you this prayer language to bring you from the realm of personal edification to building up the Body of Christ. Praying in the Spirit helps you to learn to trust God more completely. Every new phase is a fresh step of faith. The Holy Spirit empowers you in the place of prayer (see Rom. 8:26).

Because he constantly engaged in praying in the Spirit (see 1 Cor. 14:18-19), Paul stayed empowered by the Holy Spirit. Because he kept in touch with the Spirit, his faith shone red hot for God. Praying in the Spirit is your God-given privilege and a winning ticket to ever-increasing faith. It will help you arise from any form of religion that is crippling you and help you engage yourself in godly, faith-building exercise.

Pray this prayer:

Father God, I know without faith it is impossible to please You. Help me to keep my faith alive and active. I will pray daily in the Spirit so that my faith can grow a little stronger each time. In Jesus' name, amen.

CHAPTER ELEVEN

The Wonders of Divine Direction

Prayer is an avenue to receive divine direction.

A young man discovered a vein of gold high in the mountains, but he struggled mightily to develop it. His tireless efforts led nowhere and he repeatedly failed. One night as he rested after a long, hard day, he muttered, "I know what my difficulty is; I don't know anything about this rock. I don't know anything about geology or mining. So, I'm going to the city to find out."

Heading down from the mountains, he visited the head of the mining department at that area's university and shared his story. The professor called a mining engineer, who met with the young man. After again sharing his story, the engineer replied, "I must go see this vein." It took about a week for them to reach the isolated find, but after inspecting it, the engineer said, "There are potentially millions here. However, it will cost a great deal to get here and develop it. You will have to organize a stock company or sell it. Which will you do?"

"I am going to develop it," the young man replied.

Though it took a year of hard training and study, he devoted himself to the task. Through the long winter months he kept driving himself until, by the following spring, he had acquired the knowledge that he needed. He had to follow up this education with more hours of difficult work, but in the end his decision to pursue the development of this gold netted him millions of dollars.[1]

This story illustrates the role of direction in fulfilling God's plan for your life. This young man discovered a great asset, which I call the plan of God. He had vision. Still, he needed wisdom to fulfill that vision. He needed divine direction—to know God's way. While it took time to train himself to acquire the needed knowledge, this effort brought him accomplishment and fulfillment. Sadly, many believers are motionless physically and spiritually because they lack clear-cut direction. Knowing where you are going does not guarantee getting to your destination. It also takes the knowledge of how to get there.

With divine direction, you will know the right way to attain your vision. If God has given you a task to do, it will require His direction to reach it. He needs to lead you as He did the children of Israel:

> *The Lord took His people as His share, the people of Jacob as His very own. He found them in a desert, a windy, empty land. He surrounded them and brought them up, guarding them as those He loved very much. He was like an eagle building its nest that flutters over its young. It spreads its wings to catch them and carries them on its feathers. The Lord alone led them, and there was no foreign god helping Him. The Lord brought them to the heights of the land and fed them the fruit of the fields. He gave them honey from the rocks, bringing oil from the solid rock* (Deuteronomy 32:9-13).

It is one thing to know what you want in life as part of God's divine plan, but it is another to know how to get what you want. The wonder of God leading you is one of the greatest things that can happen to a believer. The Creator of the world has a perfect understanding of your life and is interested in guiding you to your Promised Land. However, you have a personal responsibility to wait before Him, seeking direction in His Word and prayer. Declare as David did, *"You will teach me how to live a holy life. Being with You will fill me with joy; at Your right hand I will find pleasure forever"* (Ps. 16:11).

The Right Directions

I once took a journey that should have required about five hours, but I wound up on the road for eight. Near the end of my journey, the road map I was following guided me in the wrong direction. Because of that, I wound up driving in circles, trying to determine the correct route to my final destination. Though I thought I knew where I was going, my lack of understanding of exactly how to get there meant it took three hours longer than expected.

Many men have the reputation of refusing to ask for directions while they are driving. They don't like to admit that they don't know something. Instead of asking for help, such people prefer to drive aimlessly for hours, thinking they will somehow stumble onto the right answer. The method of going in circles may work if you have a general knowledge of the area, but if you must reach a specific destination in a strange town, you need the right directions. Ask God for help: *"This is what the Lord says: 'Stand where the roads cross and look. Ask where the old way is, where the good way is, and walk on it. If you do, you will find rest for yourselves'"* (Jer. 6:16).

While it may seem that God has something specific set aside for you to do, first you must seek His guidance. It is impossible to arrive safely at God's destination for your life if you don't consult the only One who can see where you are going. God is committed to showing you the way: *"You will show me the path of life; in Your presence is fullness of joy; at Your right hand are pleasures forevermore"* (Ps. 16:11 NKJV).

Divine direction is a major prerequisite for success. While it is a God-given privilege for a believer, in order to enjoy it you must seek it through prayer and Bible study. God's ways of carrying out His will for your life is not something that you discover "out there," through trial and error. It is something you will find "in Him" through a diligent, earnest life of prayer. Only those who determine to ask God for His help will discover the right path, the way that leads to the fulfillment of a colorful destiny. You will never reach your God-given destiny walking on the wrong path. Your soul will never find rest or reach your vision outside of God's roadmap.

God's Roadmap

God's roadmap is in the person of Jesus. He told His disciples, *"I am the way, and the truth, and the life. The only way to the Father is through Me"* (John 14:6). Trying to accomplish your vision without a commitment to Christ through the fellowship of prayer and studying His Word will lead to hopelessness. It is too risky for you to go through life, doing what seems right, without making a commitment to seeking God's roadmap. His commitment to direct you will amount to nothing if you don't ask Him to guide you. Prayer will help you eliminate possible missteps by replacing them with God's perfect steps to accomplish your dream. As you give yourself to a lifestyle of fellowship with Christ through prayer and studying His Word, the Lord—through His Spirit—will lead you into green pastures:

> *The Lord is my shepherd; I shall not want. He makes me to lie down in green pastures; He leads me beside the still waters. He restores my soul; He leads me in the paths of righteousness for His name's sake. Yea,*

> *though I walk through the valley of the shadow of death, I will fear no evil; for You are with me; Your rod and Your staff, they comfort me. You prepare a table before me in the presence of my enemies; You anoint my head with oil; my cup runs over* (Psalm 23:1-5 NKJV).

God's roadmap guarantees provision, peace, and protection from the devil. When God leads you, He makes crooked paths straight and rough places plain. Your prayer to Him should always be, *"Cause me to hear Your lovingkindness in the morning, for in You do I trust; cause me to know the way in which I should walk, for I lift up my soul to You"* (Ps. 143:8 NKJV).

Following Christ will position you to receive divine direction. When the Israelites came out of slavery and bondage in Egypt, they didn't know exactly where they were going. They just knew they had been promised that Canaan was a land flowing with milk and honey. Even their leaders, Moses and Aaron, weren't sure of the route. When they set out across the dessert on their journey, God alone knew the way. He led them by a pillar of cloud during the day and fire by night. With these symbols, they knew when to move and when to remain in camp. Moses constantly stayed in God's presence, receiving divine direction for leading the people.

Ignorance limits people, which limits what God can do with them. Those who will receive quality instruction in these perilous times are those led by God. Hearing His voice requires spending quality time in His presence. It reminds me of the evangelist who said, "I don't try to solve every problem I see in ministry. All I do is listen to the voice of the Holy Spirit to know which problem requires my attention. I learn to put my ear in the mouth of God."

More than ever, today the Church needs a profound conviction of the vast importance of prayer in carrying out its work. The early Church constantly stayed in touch with the Holy Spirit to obtain directions on how to carry out the work of ministry. The people who will be conspicuous and imposing in these final days are people who commit themselves to put their ears to the mouth of God so they can receive divine direction. They hear like Isaiah, who wrote, *"This is what the Lord, who saves you, the Holy One of Israel, says: 'I am the Lord your God, who teaches you to do what is good, who leads you in the way you should go"* (Isa. 48:17).

If you set out on the wrong way when you are driving, no matter how fast you drive you will never reach your destination because you are headed in the wrong direction. It is dangerous to ever step out without obtaining adequate direction from God. He is willing to teach us the right way to fulfill His plan if we will ask Him in prayer. Once you know the correct route, you will not fall into any ditches or get stranded. As David said,

> *The Lord says, "I will make you wise and show you where to go. I will guide you and watch over you. So don't be like a horse or donkey, that doesn't understand. They must be led with bits and reins, or they will not come near you"* (Psalm 32:8-9).

You need divine direction because misdirection can lead to years of setbacks and even wipe out your destiny. Remember, you are a son or daughter of God, not a foolish horse. Engage God through prayer so you can receive instructions regarding wise steps to take in pursuing your vision. David made divine direction his lifetime companion. He never attacked an enemy or made a move without first asking God. In Ecclesiastes, Solomon wrote,

> *If the ax is dull, and one does not sharpen the edge, then he must use more strength; but wisdom brings success....The labor of fools wearies them, for they do not even know how to go to the city!* (Ecclesiastes 10:10,15 NKJV)

This analysis reveals that lack of direction is the reason for much of the frustration that many suffer today in trying to fulfill their callings.

Receiving Divine Direction

When King Jehoshaphat faced a tough situation, he turned to God for help. The Lord responded,

> *"You will not need to fight in this battle. Position yourselves, stand still and see the salvation of the Lord, who is with you, O Judah and Jerusalem!" Do not fear or be dismayed; tomorrow go out against them, for the Lord is with you* (2 Chronicles 20:17 NKJV).

The victory recorded in this chapter came as a result of the divine instruction Jehoshaphat received for the people of Judah. Through this king and prophet, God instructed them to set themselves, stand still, and watch to see the Lord's salvation. To set yourself means to position yourself in the right place so you can see victory. It is similar to acting like the moon, which has no light of its own. All it does is position itself at a particular angle to the sun and the sun's rays at night. It is impossible for the moon to shine unless it positions itself at the right place. As it is in the natural, so it is in the spiritual. You must be in a covenant position to gain access to God's voice and leading.

What are these covenant positions?

Be a Sheep-Minded Believer

God commits Himself to lead those willing to become like sheep in His hands. While I don't have space to review all the characteristics of sheep, one of their distinctive qualities that makes them a perfect example is the relationship between the sheep and the shepherd. A sheep has the ability to recognize the voice of its shepherd and be loyal to his instructions as he leads the herd to green pastures.

Jesus illustrated this when He told the disbelieving Pharisees,

> *The one who guards the door opens it for him. And the sheep listen to the voice of the shepherd. He calls his own sheep by name and leads them out. When he brings all his sheep out, he goes ahead of them, and they follow him because they know his voice. But they will never follow a stranger. They will run away from him because they don't know his voice....I am the good shepherd. The good shepherd gives His life for the sheep* (John 10:3-5,11).

God only gives instructions to sheep, not goats. Until you make up your mind to be loyal and faithful to the written Word of God and prayer, you can never become a sheep-minded believer. When sheep are in close proximity to the Shepherd, who is Jesus Christ, it makes it easy for them to know His voice. Many Christians want God's direction for their lives, but are not willing to commit themselves to a lifestyle of prayer and fellowship with His Word. Only in the place of prayer will your heart become like a sheep's.

King David said in Psalm 23:1, *"The Lord is my shepherd...."* David was a shepherd boy when the Lord called and anointed him king over Israel. This gave him keen understanding of how to relate to the Lord, the Master Shepherd. The covenant position of being a sheep-minded believer made David a triumphant warrior. Want victory in life? Learn to act as David did.

Be Soft and Pliable

Being soft and pliable means becoming flexible in God's hands. Being full of your own desires, thoughts, and schemes disqualifies you from discerning God's ways and plans for your life. You can't come to God with selfish motives and expect God to give you divine direction. God gave this word to the prophet Jeremiah:

> *For thus says the Lord to the men of Judah and Jerusalem: "Break up your fallow ground, and do not sow among thorns. Circumcise yourselves to the Lord, and take away the foreskins of your hearts..."* (Jeremiah 4:3-4 NKJV).

When your heart is not soft and pliable, it is like fallow ground—land that has been plowed, but not seeded, and is inactive, with thorns on it. Like seeds that can't sprout in this infertile soil, God's Word cannot grow in a hard heart. To gain access to the Spirit's voice for clear direction, you need to become tender in His hands. You need to pray, "Not my will, Lord, but Your will be done in my life," even when it's tough to do the will of God. This is what Jesus prayed when He was facing imminent death on the cross: *"Father, if it is Your will, take this cup away from Me; nevertheless not My will, but Yours, be done"* (Luke 22:42 NKJV).

Be Determined to Be Led by God

I used the word *be* to show you the covenant position necessary to receive divine direction. What you are is a starting point to what you become. It is your state of being that ultimately registers your status in life. Be determined to be led by God alone, and let nothing in this life pull you away from this state of being. The person with determination possesses a driving force that will keep him or her focused on God's desires. Determination will drive you to the presence of God in prayer so that you can receive divine direction. David demonstrated this kind of determination when he wrote in the Psalms, *"I have stuck unto Thy testimonies: O Lord, put me not to shame"* (Ps. 119:31 KJV).

It takes determination to stick to something. People of determination are people who refuse to be distracted in their pursuits, even under strong pressure. Like David, you must choose to stick to the habit of constantly inquiring of the Lord: *"I have inclined my heart to perform Your statutes forever, to the very end"* (Ps. 119:112 NKJV). It takes determination to do the same thing repeatedly and to stay with it throughout your life. David's declaration can be summed up: "I will not just perform God's statutes, but I will stay with it until my life is over." This is determination at work. Your ability to receive and obey divine instruction will ultimately determine how much of God's will you are able to fulfill in your life.

This is why evangelists like Charles G. Finney left such a shining legacy. So strong was the determination and passion of this great revivalist that he engaged in agonizing prayer. So passionate were his prayers that the Holy Spirit stirred people to repent before he arrived for his meetings, leading to a wave of conversions across the cities where he spoke. This is the power of determination that produces travailing prayer—the kind that goes beyond the power of the flesh. It loses its focus on time, tiredness, and public opinion. The key element in success is determination. My experience in ministry has led me to the conclusion that habit will take people deeper in God than their desire, but it takes strong determination to form a habit of prayer.

Be Meek

In the Sermon on the Mount, Jesus lauded this quality: *"Blessed are the meek, for they shall inherit the earth"* (Matt. 5:5 NKJV). Later, He told a multitude, *"Take My yoke upon you and learn of Me; for I am meek and lowly in heart and you shall find rest unto your souls"* (Matt. 11:29 NKJV).

Meekness is not what you do or what you wear, it is who you are. Talking one day with my spiritual father, Bishop Bart Pierce of Rock City Church in Baltimore, Maryland, I asked him about some of his secrets to success. Among the keys he shared was his ability to listen and receive instruction from people above him in ministry. This is an acid test of meekness because it takes humility to receive instruction from others. A humble person is a teachable person, and a teachable person is a humble person. God takes such special delight in the meek that He has reserved the earth for them. Your destiny here cannot become outstanding and conspicuous if you lack a spirit of meekness. Since only the meek will possess the earth, it stands to reason that without meekness you cannot fulfill your mission.

Meekness is not weakness, but complete dependence on God and His ways. It is personified by a lowliness of heart. There are some people who may appear to be humble, yet secretly are arrogant in their hearts. Instead, you should strive to be like Moses. According to Numbers 12:3, Moses was the meekest man on the earth at that time. Verse 8 in the same chapter tells us that God spoke to him *"mouth to mouth"* (KJV).

Despite being on such a high level of proximity with God, Moses still received the instruction from his father-in-law, Jethro, when he advised him to stop trying to judge all the sticky disputes and cases that arose in Israel. Warning Moses that he would wear himself out, Jethro told him to appoint

> *...officers over the people, to rule over groups of thousands, hundreds, fifties, and tens. Let these officers solve the disagreements among the people all the time. They can bring the hard cases to you, but they can decide the simple cases themselves. That will make it easier for you, because they will share the work with you* (Exodus 18:21-22).

Moses followed this wise counsel. His action stemmed from his heart of meekness. How can a man who speaks to God Almighty face-to-face receive instruction and direction from an ordinary man? Meekness. When you possess this spirit, you aren't afraid to admit you are incapable in some area and are willing to allow God to supply you with His capability, which brings you the results you seek.

Amazing wonders are about to be revealed on the earth. Only people who know the ways of God will participate in these wonders. Only those who are meek are qualified to receive His direction; only those who admit that they don't know everything will receive His revelation. David once said, *"The meek will He guide in judgment: and the meek will He teach His way"* (Ps. 25:9 KJV). Those who think they know everything actually don't know anything! Thinking you are beyond instruction shuts the door to receiving divine direction from God. Self must give way before meekness can show itself. Meekness strategically positions you in the place to connect to the voice of Heaven. God is committed to guiding you and bringing you into your Promised Land, but you must prove to Him that you are meek enough to receive His instruction.

What guarantees certainty in an uncertain world is your ability to receive divine direction. Ask yourself: "Am I living by trial and error or by the instruction of God's Word?" God has not ordained that you live by endless, backbreaking labor, toil, and worry. Instead, He wants you to live by the Word that comes from His mouth. This is what Jesus said when He rebuffed the first of satan's trio of temptations: *"It is written, 'Man shall not live by bread alone, but by every word that proceeds from the mouth of God"* (Matt. 4:4 NKJV).

Pray this prayer:

Lord, You have the right road map for the fulfillment of Your vision for my life. I commit myself to always seek direction from You. Holy Spirit, give me the mind of a sheep and make my heart flexible, willing, and meek, enabling me to receive divine direction. In Jesus' name, amen.

Endnote

1. E.W. Kenyon, *Signposts on the Road to Success* (Lynnwood, WA: Kenyon's Gospel Publishing Society, 1983), 36-37.

CHAPTER TWELVE

The Wonders of Divine Intimacy

Prayer is the place of building friendship and relationship with God.

Invited to speak at an Assembly of God church in the Baltimore area not too long ago, I invested time in Scripture study and prayer so I would be prepared to relate God's message to the people. One day, as I prayed, the Holy Spirit told me, "When you go to this church, you will meet a woman named Elizabeth. I want you to speak to her." This message assured me that I was on God's mission. In John 15:15, Jesus told His disciples:

> *I no longer call you servants, because a servant does not know what his master is doing. But I call you friends, because I have made known to you everything I heard from My Father.*

While I drove to this speaking engagement with my two assistants, the Spirit reminded me to speak to Elizabeth that day—even though He didn't tell me what I was to say to her.

Confident that He would reveal that to me at the right time, I spoke that day about experiencing personal revival. As I was about to wrap up my message, the Spirit again brought "Elizabeth" to mind. After I finished speaking, I invited people who wanted prayer and a fresh touch from God to come forward.

As people started walking to the front, I thought about speaking out Elizabeth's name. Then I hesitated, thinking, "If I call her name and nobody comes, I'm going to make a fool of myself." Suddenly, faith leaped in my spirit and I heard the Spirit whisper, "I will give you the word for her when she comes." That summoned my courage. I told the congregation, "Is somebody named Elizabeth here? Where are you? The Holy Spirit told me somebody named Elizabeth should come forth."

Silence. The next minute seemed to drag like an hour. Finally, an African woman rose from a seat in the back. When she got to the altar, I asked, "Are you Elizabeth?"

"Yes."

I didn't learn her whole story until after I had prayed with her. As we prayed, I declared that she didn't need to worry any longer about the immigration authorities. Just then, I sensed the Spirit telling me to take the glass of water that had been poured for me to use during my sermon and give it to her. Water is symbolic of the Holy Spirit and the Word of God (see Isa. 55.10-11). The reason I did it was following the prompting of the Holy Spirit. Her receiving the water was an act of faith indicating that she received the prophetic word into her heart. When I did, she started crying. It turns out she was scheduled for an immigration hearing in the near future and was about to be deported to Nigeria. The day before, she had asked a friend from this church if her husband could find her a good immigration lawyer. He had told her that the situation was so far advanced that there weren't any attorneys who could help her. But, he said, a guest speaker was going to be at their church the next day if she could come. Like me, it would be her first time in this church.

A month later, the man who introduced me to this church met the husband of the woman who had invited the Nigerian lady. He shared the thrilling conclusion to this story. The day after I prayed for the Nigerian native, the immigration service had called. They told her she no longer had to worry about deportation because that order had been lifted. Instead, they invited her to come to their offices to apply for her green card, signifying permanent residency. My heart leaped for joy, both for her and for my friendship with God. He had told me what He was going to do before He did it, then followed through by keeping His promise.

"Show Me Your Friends"

Americans like to say, "Show me your friends and I will tell you who you are." Whoever came up with this statement understands the powerful impact of friends. Friends become that way through forming a close, intimate relationship. They become so used to each other they often reason alike and act in similar ways. The idea of friendship originated with God. In his plea for help as he faced battle, Jehoshaphat asked, *"Are You not our God, who drove out the inhabitants of this land before Your people Israel, and gave it to the descendants of Abraham Your friend forever?"* (2 Chron. 20:7 NKJV). James wrote, *"And the Scripture was fulfilled which says, 'Abraham believed God, and it was accounted to him for righteousness.' And he was called the friend of God"* (James 2:23 NKJV).

The Bible defines friendship as a close, trusting relationship between two people. Abraham developed his relationship with God through diligent obedience to His voice. A close look at Abraham's life reveals that he was a man of prayer. His lifelong fellowship with God built this relationship to the level that he became a friend with a keen understanding of what God will and will not do. He knew God's mind when the Lord tested him and told him to offer his only son, Isaac, as a burnt offering (see Gen. 22:1-18). Abraham knew God so well that he reasoned that even if God took Isaac's life, He could raise him from the dead (see Heb. 11:17-19).

Abraham didn't have this kind of rock-solid trust when God called him to leave Haran and go to Canaan (see Gen. 12). In the process of time—through fellowship and relationship with God, prayer, and obedience—Abraham came to the level of a willingness to sacrifice his future (Isaac) for God. The test of your friendship with God is whether you are willing to lay down what is precious in your heart.

Nobody can arrive at this level of intimacy in a short amount of time. It takes effort to build a relationship to the level of trusting one's life to another person. This is why a lifestyle of prayer and obedience to God's Word is so significant. Only in the place of prayer will your friendship with God develop. As Abraham walked with God, His nature—which is faith—rubbed off on Abraham. *If you don't learn to spend time with God in prayer, you will never be able to listen to His voice and obey Him in every issue of life.*

Jesus connects friendship with prayer. His choosing of His disciples seems to have occurred with the thought in mind that they would bear fruit through prayer.

> *You are My friends if you do what I command you. I no longer call you servants, because a servant does not know what his master is doing. But I call you friends, because I have made known to you everything I heard from My Father* (John 15:14-15).

You cannot disassociate prayer from intimacy with God and bearing fruit. Verse 16 adds, *"You did not choose Me; I chose you. And I gave you this work: to go and produce fruit, fruit that will last. Then the Father will give you anything you ask for in My name."*

The problem with today's Church does not start with the devil, but with a lack of commitment to prayer. Many believers cannot give an accurate account of how they spend the 168 hours in their week. A majority only give God two or three hours. It is no wonder we have so many powerless, unproductive Christians. Such folks cannot hang their lives on what they claim to believe because they have no relationship with the God they claim to follow. God's nature, character, and lifestyle that should shine through believers is not visible to the world because they don't exercise the power of prayer.

In Christ's Presence

The disciples carried the reputation of Christ's friends:

> *The leaders saw that Peter and John were not afraid to speak, and they understood that these men had no special training or education. So they were amazed. Then they realized that Peter and John had been with Jesus* (Acts 4:13).

My spiritual father, Bishop Bart Pierce, often says, "A man with an experience is never at the mercy of a man with an argument." Judging from the above passage, this statement is true. After seeing the miracle Peter and John performed, those who wanted to stifle the Gospel couldn't cite any evidence against them. They concluded they had been with Jesus, which is what empowered them to speak and act with such authority.

Although Jesus was no longer present physically with them, Peter and John were among the disciples who spent time with

Christ in prayer, including after the outpouring of the Holy Spirit described in Acts 2. Afterward, they performed the attention-getting miracle of healing a lame beggar (see Acts 3) while on their way to the temple to spend time with Jesus. These disciples were in the habit of praying because they understood through their experience with their Master that prayer is the key to building friendship with God. Developing that friendship forms intimacy, which produces power.

Samuel Shoemaker, the Episcopal priest instrumental in helping write Alcoholics Anonymous' founding principles, once said, "Prayer may not always change things for you, but it will change you for things."[1] Prayer changed Peter and John forever. Because of their lifestyle of prayer, Peter could boldly proclaim to a lame beggar, *"I don't have any silver or gold, but I do have something else I can give you. By the power of Jesus Christ from Nazareth, stand up and walk"* (Acts 3:6). Though not rich in monetary terms, these disciples had something money could not buy—the name of Jesus Christ of Nazareth. This gave them an advantage over every circumstance. Their commitment to prayer enabled them to become the living Christ to their world.

His name is not a magic coin that anyone can use to release power. Many Christians call on Jesus' name, but don't see God's power released because they lack a close relationship with Him. Likewise, many people want to reign with Jesus in power and glory, but they don't want to embrace His full image, which includes identifying with His suffering. As Paul wrote to Timothy, *"This teaching is true: If we died with Him, we will also live with Him. If we accept suffering, we will also rule with Him. If we say we don't know Him, He will say He doesn't know us"* (2 Tim. 2:11-12).

Identifying with Christ starts with prayer, which is grueling work. It is where the flesh dies and the spirit within a believer comes alive with God. This is one of the reasons satan fights so hard to cut off our communication with Heaven. The devil is willing to pay any price to hinder prayer. He knows that where people build intimacy with God, it will produce power to destroy the devil's work. As long as you lack an intimate relationship with the God of the Church, the enemy is not threatened by your involvement in church activities.

The thing that satan dreads above everything is dedicated, sincere prayer. Those who have the spirit of prayer carry the influence of Heaven, where matters concerning life are determined. The Friend you spend much time with will ultimately determine the spiritual influence you possess. Satan was behind the men who wanted to stop the spread of the Gospel. But they recognized Peter and John had been with Jesus. Once believers build up their relationships with God through prayer, they will become threats to the kingdom of darkness.

From Fellowship to Relationship

Fellowship with God determines the level of your relationship with Him. This is why Jesus said *"that men always ought to pray and not lose heart"* (Luke 18:1 NKJV). And it's why Paul taught the Church to *"pray continually"* (1 Thess. 5:17). Prayer is the medium of a relationship with God that gives birth to intimacy. The more you fellowship with God in prayer, the closer your relationship and the more intimate you become. You build any relationship through constant contact and interaction—without it, it is impossible to claim one. Broken fellowship leads to broken relationships and friendships, which leads to loss of authority and power. Adam and Eve lost their right to reign on earth because they broke their fellowship with God (see Gen. 3:1-12).

Prayer is the communication line that God gives to believers to enable them to fellowship with the divine. Once your communication lines are cut, your fellowship is destroyed. Then you become vulnerable to the devil's attacks. Most problems in the Body of Christ come from broken fellowship. Jesus showed us how to maintain it. Before His crucifixion, Jesus told His disciples, *"I will no longer talk much with you, for the ruler of this world is coming, and he has nothing in Me* (John 14:30 NKJV). This was a bold statement, meaning that nothing associated with satan had any connection with Christ. It couldn't, because He stayed in touch with His Father through prayer. When believers don't embrace a lifestyle of prayer, they become magnets for every satanic missile flying around the atmosphere.

When the enemy strikes, will he find something in you that makes him want to turn back? Or will he stay because he sees that you are prayerless and trying to do everything in your own power? This is a serious question that you need to ponder. The quality of your fellowship with the Lord through prayer will determine the level of your relationship. I have known the Lord for more than 22 years, many of them as an independent missionary with no visible means of financial support. I started my ministry in Africa and later migrated to America, and through all those years, God has been faithful as I follow His leading through worship and prayer. In the decade since I came to the United States, I have never run out of resources to meet my needs. To the human mind, this may sound risky. But in the spiritual realm, it is the safest place to be—as long as I remain in touch with God and listen to His voice.

One necessary quality of friendship is how it sharpens our mind and senses. Wise Solomon wrote, *"As iron sharpens iron, so a man sharpens the countenance of his friend"* (Prov. 27:17 NKJV). Likewise, in prayer your relationship with God is sharpened while your spirit is renewed with the glory of His presence. When iron is sharpened, it produces better results.

Fellowship with the Lord will sharpen you, enabling you to attract the favor of God and people. It will also enhance your personality since those who spend time fellowshipping with God carry His nature with them.

Moses Camped With God

So he was there with the Lord forty days and forty nights; he neither ate bread nor drank water. And He wrote on the tablets the words of the covenant, the Ten Commandments. Now it was so, when Moses came down from Mount Sinai (and the two tablets of the Testimony were in Moses' hand when he came down from the mountain), that Moses did not know that the skin of his face shone while he talked with Him. So when Aaron and all the children of Israel saw Moses, behold, the skin of his face shone, and they were afraid to come near him (Exodus 34:28-30 NKJV).

When Moses camped with God on Mount Sinai, he came away carrying His glory. Until your hunger to be changed into the likeness of God exceeds your hunger to be successful in life or ministry, you cannot carry the kind of glory that rested on Moses. God has committed all His glory in His Son,

Who, being the brightness of His glory and the express image of His person, and upholding all things by the word of His power, when He had by Himself purged our sins, sat down at the right hand of the Majesty on high (Hebrews 1:3 NKJV).

Fellowship with Jesus makes you a partaker of this glory. Only in the place of prayer can you strengthen your relationship with Him and manifest His glory. The world is desperately looking for such people.

Would you be the one to show the world God's glory? It takes intimacy with Him to represent Him in body, soul, and spirit. A distant relationship will never produce intimacy. How can you feel the heartbeat of a man if you are not close to his heart? Intimacy requires nearness, which requires a commitment to fellowship and relationship with God through prayer. Jesus connects abiding in Him with prayer. *"If you abide in Me, and My words abide in you, you will ask what you desire, and it shall be done for you"* (John 15:7 NKJV).

You can never tell what a person is made of, or what he or she can or can't do, until you spend enough time fellowshipping and relating with that person. The problem with the Church today is that many people in the Body of Christ don't know the Christ of the Body. This lack of knowledge, which is caused by lack of fellowship and relationship, causes weakness. Even Paul, after more than 25 years in ministry, cried out for a deeper, more intimate walk with Jesus, *"that I may know Him and the power of His resurrection, and the fellowship of His sufferings, being conformed to His death"* (Phil. 3:10 NKJV). If a man like Paul could be so hungry for a deeper walk of intimacy, you need the same kind of appetite.

Proximity Produces Penetration

Enoch was a remarkable man, one so close to God that he walked off this earth and into Heaven (see Gen. 5:24). Enoch was a descendant of Enosh, the son of Seth (Seth was the son of Adam and Eve who took Abel's place after Cain killed Abel). Enosh advocated prayer and restored fellowship with God through prayer; after his birth *"people began to pray to the Lord"* (Gen. 4:26). I believe Enosh and those who followed him passed down this hunger for intimacy with God to Enoch, part of the seventh generation from Adam. Enoch walked with God so closely he changed into God's likeness and conquered physical death.

The close walk that Enoch enjoyed with God should be your goal. At some point in your life, you need to ask yourself: Am I walking with God or am I walking for God? It takes effective, diligent fellowship in prayer to build a relationship that makes you follow God's plan for your life. The closer your walk with Him, the easier it becomes for His Spirit to penetrate your heart so you will follow His ways. Recently, as I was sitting and talking with God at home, the Holy Spirit spoke to my spirit, saying, "Not all good works My people do in the Kingdom are approved by Me. Only those things that are done by faith in accordance to My instruction are approved by Me." This statement sank deep into my spirit and quenched every personal ambition I had about ministry.

Sometimes we look at people's achievements in life and conclude that they have fulfilled their destiny, but that is not necessarily true in God's sight. It takes an intimate walk with God to produce His results. That will determine how much of His will you are able to fulfill while you are on this earth. Every child of God's Kingdom receives a divine assignment when he or she is born again. The ability to fulfill that assignment rests on whether or not a person walks closely with God. David is a shining example of someone who understood this vital relationship. More than half of the book of Psalms is dedicated to his prayers and praises. They brim with such statements as *"Seven times a day I praise You, because of Your righteous judgments"* (Ps. 119:164 NKJV) and *"Evening and morning and at noon I will pray, and cry aloud, and He shall hear my voice"* (Ps. 55:17 NKJV).

David praised God seven times a day and prayed three times a day. This shows the type of closeness he had with the Lord. David never embarked in battle without first seeking God's direction. One example of this occurred when the Philistines were making a raid on a nearby valley:

> *Therefore David inquired again of God, and God said to him, "You shall not go up after them; circle around them, and come upon them in front of the mulberry trees"* (1 Chronicles 14:14 NKJV).

The fact that David "inquired again" of God indicates he had asked Him before, which shows how closely David stayed in touch with the Lord. Only those who will possess this kind of spirit of prayer will arrive at a greater level of intimacy. The Bible states that through a life of prayer, David accomplished God's will to the fullest capacity (see Acts 13:22,36). Tenderness of heart and transformation of mind come in the place of proximity. The closer you are to God, the more you change into His image:

> *Our faces, then, are not covered. We all show the Lord's glory, and we are being changed to be like Him. This change in us brings ever greater glory, which comes from the Lord, who is the Spirit* (2 Corinthians 3:18).

Is God calling you into a closer walk with Him? You will never experience the reality of His presence in your daily life until you make up your mind to avoid passivity in your prayer life and make a daily appointment with God. Andrew Murray once said, "Those who do not have a set time to pray do not."[2] Strive to be like Daniel, the prophet who was on intimate terms with the Lord. He developed this relationship to the point that his prayer life brought about an "open Heaven" in the strange land called Babylon. Daniel prayed to the point that Heaven released angels to his prayer closet (see Dan. 9:20–10:21). This closeness came from his daily prayer appointments.

Daniel never neglected prayer, even when it gave his adversaries the ability to locate him and bring charges against him to King Darius (see Dan. 6:1-23). Daniel prayed three times a day. So great was his relationship with God that even hungry lions could not devour him. I pray that the Holy Spirit would bring you and me into the kind of intimacy where we become a wonder to our generation. My prayer has always been, *"I have become as a wonder to many, but You are my strong refuge"* (Ps. 71:7 NKJV). May this be your prayer as well.

From City of Blood to City of Revival

Benin City, Nigeria, where I grew up, was once known as the city of blood, a gruesome place where idol worshipers used human beings for sacrifice. These pagans lived in almost every part of the city. In this West African city in the early 1970s, God raised up a man called Benson Idahosa. He was so in touch with God that Heaven pushed back the forces of darkness. A great revival broke out across the city and throughout Nigeria. The revival expanded to the point that people were flocking to Benin City from overseas to experience the movement at Idahosa's church, the Miracle Centre. Its annual camp meeting attracted believers from America and other nations of the world. I personally am a product of that great revival.

Today, the city once known as the city of blood has been transformed to the city of revival because a man touched Heaven and brought down its domain to earth. Though Idahosa died in 1998, the effect of his intimate relationship with God is felt today, both in Nigeria and across the world. You can read the life story of this great apostle of faith and prayer in the book *Fire in His Bones.*[3]

Benson's prayer life was as earnest, needy, and hungry as a starving child's cry for bread. The wonders of intimacy with God spring from this kind of prayer life. It drives the prayer to want to be in God's presence, building friendship and relationship. The world is looking and waiting for people who can, by their relationship with the invisible God, make Him a visible reality in the world. Would you be the one who would carry the miracle power of God to this generation?

Pray this prayer:

Thank you, dear Lord, that I can have an intimate relationship with You as I devote myself to a daily appointment with You. May I never get too busy to miss my daily time of fellowship with You. In Jesus' name, amen.

Endnotes

1. See, for example, Dick B., *New Light on Alcoholism, God, Samuel Shoemaker, and AA* (Maui, HI: Paradise Research Publications, 1999), http://www.dickb.com/newlight.shtml.

2. Andrew Murray, *With Christ in the School of Prayer* (New Kensington, PA: Whitaker House, 1981).

3. Ruthanne Garlock, *Fire in His Bones: The Story of Benson Idahosa* (Tulsa, OK: Harrison House, 1986).

CHAPTER THIRTEEN

The Wonders of Miracles

Prayer is the breeding ground for miracles.

While miracles mark the supernatural intervention of God, until people pray they will not see miracles on earth. I saw the truth of this statement on a visit to Nigeria in the summer of 2006, when I had an opportunity to minister to my older brother and his wife. At that time they had been married for almost ten years without being able to conceive a child. They sought out everything they could in the natural, but without any results. One day as we talked, he sighed deeply as he said, "We have spent close to $3,000 to resolve this problem. All our efforts have been fruitless."

"I don't know why I'm going through this situation," his wife said. "We've tried everything we can think of."

They looked as helpless as if they were trying to hold a tidal wave back with their bare hands. It wasn't just the frustration of remaining childless. Their parents, friends, and other family members had been second-guessing them. My brother, who had once made a decision to follow Christ, but then drifted away from God, was even contemplating following the custom of some Nigerians and taking a second wife.

First I counseled them that they needed to return to God and rededicate their efforts to following Christ. Once they had taken that step, I opened my Bible and shared God's promise concerning fruitlessness in the area of child bearing. I showed them such passages as Exodus 23:25-26, where God tells the children of Israel,

> *If you worship the Lord your God, I will bless your bread and your water. I will take away sickness from you. None of your women will have her baby die before it is born, and all women will have children. I will allow you to live long lives.*

I showed them the place where the Israelites are getting ready to enter the Promised Land and Moses tells them if they remain faithful to God that they *"will be blessed more than any other people. Every husband and wife will have children, and all your cattle will have calves"* (Deut. 7:14).

I showed them how an angel appeared to Samson's mother and told her that though she was barren, she would give birth to a son who would deliver Israel from the hands of the Philistines (see Judg. 13:3-5). And I pointed out the Psalm that says, *"He grants the barren woman a home, like a joyful mother of children. Praise the Lord"* (Ps. 113:9 NKJV). I told them how Isaiah, soon after prophesying about Christ's suffering and crucifixion, wrote,

> *"Sing, O barren, you who have not borne! Break forth into singing, and cry aloud, you who have not labored with child! For more are the children of the desolate than the children of the married woman,"* says the Lord (Isaiah 54:1 NKJV).

I told them the story of Zacharias and Elizabeth, who were old and childless when an angel appeared to them and said,

> *Zechariah, don't be afraid. God **has heard your prayer**. Your wife, Elizabeth, will give birth to a son, and you will name him John. He will bring you joy and gladness, and many people will be happy because of his birth. John will be a great man for the Lord. He will never drink wine or beer, and even from birth, he will be filled with the Holy Spirit. He will help many people of Israel return to the Lord their God. He will go before the Lord in spirit and power like Elijah. He will make peace between parents and their children and will bring those who are not obeying God back to the right way of thinking, to make a people ready for the coming of the Lord* (Luke 1:13-17).

I ended with a Psalm:

> *Your wife shall be like a fruitful vine in the very heart of your house, your children like olive plants all around your table. Behold, thus shall the man be blessed who fears the Lord* (Psalm 128:3-4 NKJV).

These Scriptures persuaded them to believe what God said in His Word, messages they gladly received. Anointing them with oil, I prayed for them what I sensed the Holy Spirit leading me to say, "God, if I have found favor in Your sight and Your Word is true, grant them according to the season of life a child. Grant them their heart's desire."

Afterward, I told them, "You will have a baby according to the season of life"—meaning nine months. Soon after this, I returned to the United States. Three months later, as I was getting ready for a trip to India, my brother called to say his wife was about three months pregnant. Their first child was born in February of 2007.

This is the wonder of miracles. These supernatural events are one way of knowing that God in Heaven intervenes in earth's affairs and helps people. Miracles and prayer go hand in hand, as a supernatural cause-and-effect. If believers knew how to pray so they saw more answers to their prayers, they would be bolder to share their faith in Christ with others around them. The believer who lives the life of the miraculous is a person who stays in touch with God through a deliberate commitment to a prayer-filled lifestyle. Will you give yourself to prayer so God can flow His wonder-working power through you?

The fact that my brother and sister-in-law have a healthy, growing toddler is living proof that God hears and answers prayer. There are many more. One of my favorites is a story more than a century old, told by famed English preacher and author Dean Hole (1819-1904). It involved George Benfield, a conductor on the Midland Railway. One day, Benfield stood on the foot plate of the front car, oiling his engine while the train was stationary, when his foot slipped. He fell into the space between two sets of tracks. Hearing the express train coming, Benfield only had time to stretch out his six-foot frame flat as the train rushed by. Miraculously, he escaped unhurt. Later, he returned home in the middle of the night. As he was going upstairs he heard his 8-year-old daughter crying and went to her room to investigate.

"Oh Father," she said, sobbing, "I thought somebody came and told me that you were going to be killed. I got out of bed and prayed that God would not let you die."[1]

Was it only a dream—a simple "coincidence?" George Benfield and others believe that he owed his life to the prayer of his 8-year-old daughter. Her labor in the place of prayer was the breeding ground for her father's deliverance from death. If she had not prayed, God wouldn't have had anything to work with. The power of prayer moved Him to do great things.

Book of Miracles

Earlier I mentioned Acts 16, which describes how Paul and Silas prayed and sang such loud praises to God that their fellow prisoners heard them. Suddenly, a great earthquake shook the foundations of the prison, opening the doors and loosing everyone's bonds. Paul and Silas' prayer activated this miraculous deliverance. It wasn't a passive, silent type of prayer, but an enthusiastic, praise-filled request that reached Heaven's throne. *God's desire in the twenty-first century is that His Church would operate in the same frequency as the first century apostles, emitting the same kind of fire that produces undeniable results.*

Some theologians proclaim that we can believe in God and be His children, yet they oppose and deny the reality of the supernatural. I once asked a pastor who believes that miracles have ended and were only for first-century apostles to establish the Church, "How can we call ourselves a Church and not believe in healing and in miracles? I can't read four pages in the Bible without encountering miracles! And the God of the Bible is the same today as He was back then" (see Heb. 13:8).

At first, he was speechless. Finally, he said, "Well, the miracles of Jesus are measured by quality, not quantity."

"And Jesus said the works that He did we will do, and even greater works, because He goes to the Father," I replied, paraphrasing John 14:12. That ended the discussion—not surprisingly—because the Bible is a book of miracles from beginning to end:

- What kind of a Bible would we have without three Hebrew children being delivered from a fiery furnace? (See Daniel 3:28.)

- What kind of an early Church would we have without Peter raising the cripple and gathering the sick on beds and on couches in Jerusalem's streets to be healed? (See Acts 5:15.)

- What kind of an example would Paul be without healing the sick, commanding the man with crippled feet to arise, and casting out the devil from the fortune-telling woman? (See Acts 14:10; 16:18.)

- What kind of commission would we have without Christ's order to cast out devils in His name and to lay hands on the sick for their recovery? (See Mark 16:15-20.)

If you take these promises and miracles out of the Bible, what is left? What kind of preaching do we have without evidence of miracles? Today we see in churches preachers who have performance without power, information without inspiration, and theology without kneelology. Take the miraculous out of Christianity and all we have left is another religion. Christianity is not a religion; it is the life of Christ. The Bible is a book of miracles, and every miracle recorded in it has a direct link with prayer.

The disciples were people of prayer who believed in miracles. No wonder they preached with power! Not only did they speak in the heavenly language imparted by the Holy Spirit, their consistent prayer enabled the miraculous to flow through them and touch the world. We can see the results of their action, starting in Acts 4:

After they had prayed, the place where they were meeting was shaken. They were all filled with the Holy Spirit, and they spoke God's word without fear....With great power the apostles were telling people that the Lord Jesus was truly raised from the dead. And God blessed all the believers very much (Acts 4:31,33).

Then in Acts 5 we read:

And through the hands of the apostles many signs and wonders were done among the people. And they were all with one accord in Solomon's Porch.... And believers were increasingly added to the Lord, multitudes of both men and women, so that they brought the sick out into the streets and laid them on beds and couches, that at least the shadow of Peter passing by might fall on some of them (Acts 5:12, 14-15 NKJV).

Prayer is an invitation to God, and miracles are the manifestation of God's response. Miracles don't just happen— they are stimulated by prayers of faith. The extraordinary events of miracles recorded in Acts 5 wouldn't have been possible without the disciples' commitment to prayer. Multitudes were added to God's family because of signs and wonders. These apostles preached with undeniable evidence! The Gospel of the Kingdom that Jesus entrusted to His Church to preach is one that contains evidence for the nations. Only people who are dedicated to prayer and are full of faith and the power of the Holy Spirit can demonstrate God's miraculous power.

As the disciples demonstrated, one miracle is worth a thousand sermons. All Jerusalem was attracted to Peter's preaching when the crippled beggar was healed. I saw the same thing in the late 1970s when all of Ibadan, Nigeria, gave ear to the Gospel message that Oklahoma evangelist T.L. Osborn preached. In particularly, they listened after Karimu—a crippled beggar who had crawled on the ground for 30 years—was instantly healed. His case proved that Jesus Christ remains unchanged in modern times.

Representing Christ

Right before He departed for Heaven, Christ told His disciples, *"But you shall receive power when the Holy Spirit has come upon you; and you shall be witnesses to Me in Jerusalem, and in all Judea and Samaria, and to the end of the earth"* (Acts 1:8 NKJV). God did not call you to be a lawyer who goes to court to defend someone based on the law. He has called you to be witnesses who can provide evidence. A witness is a person who has seen or knows something and is, therefore, competent to testify. Lawyers often go to court to present a case, intending to win because of a solid argument. A witness goes to court to present evidence. Only those with proof win the case.

In the days in which we live, God expects you to be an able representative of Jesus. This means that those with the desire to see God are satisfied when they come in contact with you because you have answers to their questions about life. After God poured out His Spirit on the day of Pentecost, Peter told the people, *"And so you killed the One who gives life, but God raised Him from the dead. We are witnesses to this"* (Acts 3:15). Peter boldly proclaimed this because he had proof—evidence to show that Jesus is alive. God has committed Himself to His Word. All you need to do is prayerfully represent His Word and God will back it up with the miraculous.

If the Church wants to see transformation in the world, it must stop presenting Jesus to the world while failing to pray for a fresh outpouring of the Holy Spirit so it can be a living witness of God's Kingdom. The world needs the kind of proof, evidence, and substance that Jesus said would characterize believers:

> *And these signs will follow those who believe: In My name they will cast out demons; they will speak with new tongues; they will take up serpents; and if they drink anything deadly, it will by no means hurt them; they will lay hands on the sick, and they will recover* (Mark 16:17-18 NKJV).

Note carefully the phrase, *"In My name they will..."* The believer is to go in the name of Jesus. Through His Son, God has committed His name to you so that you can perform miracles and represent Christ on earth. But it takes prayer for that life-giving force to flow out of you. The name of Jesus signifies authority and power. Paul put it this way in his letter to the Philippians:

> *God made His name greater than every other name so that every knee will bow to the name of Jesus—everyone in heaven, on earth, and under the earth. And everyone will confess that Jesus Christ is Lord and bring glory to God the Father* (Philippians 2:9-11).

He did not receive power by being passive to His Father's call on His life, but by going through the agony of torture and death on the cross.

For you to use that name to represent Him, you must bear the mark of His image. The day God sees you take up the cross (see Mark 10:21) is the day Christ's power and authority will flow through you. Only in the place of prayer can you die to self and receive His strength. Only after you are intimate with God can you receive a spiritual resurrection, exercise the Lord's authority, and use the Lord's name. The greatest commitment God made to you is allowing you to use His Son's name as yours. God assumes responsibility for those who use the name of Jesus Christ. He backs them up when they use that name because He sees the cross's power in their lives.

Do you carry the mark of the cross? Many believers are not working in the miraculous because of a lack of commitment to the Word of God and prayer. How can God's power flow through you when you don't spend quality time with Him? How can God entrust His name to you and allow you to represent Him if you don't have experiential knowledge of who He is and what He can do? Laxness in your prayer life will break God's miraculous power. Moses represented all that God is after his direct encounter with Him, when God told him, *"I AM who I AM. When you go to the people of Israel, tell them, 'I AM sent me to you'"* (Exod. 3:14). The miracles Moses produced in Egypt, after he confronted the Pharaoh and told him to let God's people go, were clear evidence that God is alive. The world in which we live is in dire need of seeing the miraculous. With its modern technological wizardry, Hollywood can produce the illusion of miracles, but only a believer walking with God can produce lasting miracles. Miracles are God's deliberate acts, motivated by deliberate prayers of people hungry to demonstrate to the world that their God is alive.

Prayer Hatches Miracles

To understand how prayer gives birth to miracles we have to look at four processes, or stages, that release them. An outstanding example is the prophet Elijah on Mount Carmel, a dynamic story found in First Kings 18:1-45. The four stages this experience illustrates are:

1. Know the Promise of God

God promised Elijah that it would rain if he showed himself to King Ahab; the chapter begins, *"During the third year without rain, the Lord spoke His word to Elijah: 'Go and meet King Ahab, and I will soon send rain'"* (1 Kings 18:1). God had given His word to shut the heavens, which we know from James 5:17 was about three and a half years. For the heavens to open and yield rain, Elijah had to know God's will concerning rain. His confidence was strong when he climbed up to the top of Mount Carmel to pray; this is the same kind of assurance we should have. *"And this is the boldness we have in God's presence: that if we ask God for anything that agrees with what He wants, He hears us"* (1 John 5:14).

Because he knew God kept His promises, Elijah didn't doubt when he prayed. His knowledge that it was God's will to send rain infused him with extraordinary strength to labor in prayer. Likewise, your knowledge of God's promises and His will forms your motivation for prayer. A lack of this revelation knowledge damages your confidence. Many go to God in prayer hoping for answers, but they lack confidence in prayer. When you are not sure of what God has provided for you, how can you confidently ask for it?

2. Have Faith in the Promise

Elijah believed that what God had said He had already done (see Mark 11:22-24). When you know God's will, it activates faith. In this passage from First Kings, Elijah told Ahab to go and eat and drink because a heavy rain was coming (see 1 Kings 18:41); he told him this right after he had slain 400 prophets of Baal—but before he had prayed. Elijah declared this word because he had faith that God had already done what He promised back in verse one.

The Creator will not cheat His creatures, those who depend on His truth. Nor will God break His word to His own servant. A lack of faith in God's promises will ultimately paralyze His miracle working power. Faith is praying. You pray because you have developed your faith, based on the promise that God will answer. *"If you ask Me for anything in My name, I will do it"* (John 14:14). It isn't enough to know the promise. You must believe also in the promise if you expect to see the manifestation.

3. Ask God to Do This Promise

This third point, the "Principle of Prayer," is the major focus of this chapter. Knowing and having faith in the promise, but never speaking it out in prayer and asking God to fulfill the promise, will amount to nothing. Faith is praying. Prayer is the hand of faith stretched out to receive. *"At the same time Elijah climbed to the top of Mount Carmel, where he bent down to the ground with his head between his knees"* (1 Kings 18:42). Elijah kneeling and putting his face between his knees represents prayer. He was out for an answer. This wasn't guess work.

As Elijah labored in prayer, he told God to do what He promised. I believe his prayer went like this: "Send the rain, oh Lord." Because he believed in God's promise, he was ready to stay there and hang on until the answer came. Until you engage the Lord in fervent prayer concerning His promise, there will be no miracle. God is waiting for your word in prayer before He releases the miracle; He doesn't work alone, and He doesn't give you what you don't ask for in prayer. *"Ask, and God will give to you. Search, and you will find. Knock, and the door will open for you"* (Matt. 7:7).

4. Act as if You Have Received His Promise

Action is the final process to the birth of a miracle.

> *Then Elijah said to his servant, "Go and look toward the sea." The servant went and looked. "I see nothing," he said. Elijah told him to go and look again. This happened seven times. The seventh time, the servant*

said, "I see a small cloud, the size of a human fist, coming from the sea." Elijah told the servant, "Go to Ahab and tell him to get his chariot ready and go home now. Otherwise, the rain will stop him" (1 Kings 18:43-44).

Sending his servant seven times to look toward the sea was an act of faith. Faith is a fact, but also an act. You can't just talk about faith; you must do the work of faith. Elijah was demonstrating his belief in the promise of rain, acting as if he had received it. One of the final verses in this passage says, *"After a short time the sky was covered with dark clouds. The wind began to blow, and soon a heavy rain began to fall..."* (1 Kings 18:45). The miracle only happened because Elijah backed up his prayer with corresponding action. This action was in mutual agreement with his prayer of faith. If you want to see the birth of a miracle in your own life, you must line up your action with your confession.

You can't be praying for something God has promised in His Word and act differently after prayer. If your action is contrary to your prayer, you disqualify yourself from seeing a miracle. For example, if you pray that there would be no rain and afterward walk around with an umbrella in your hand, you have shown that you didn't believe. Contrary to your prayer, the umbrella indicates that you are expecting it to rain. Your action has disqualified you from giving birth to your miracle.

Elijah was not into guesswork when he prayed for rain—he believed God all the way. This kind of prayer guaranteed the birth of a miracle. If people will pray as they ought to pray and back up their prayer with corresponding action, the signs, wonders, and miracles of the past will be reproduced today. When that happens, the Gospel will advance with more speed and power than it has ever known.

Pray this prayer:

I acknowledge, Father God, that You are the God of miracles and that You have sent the Holy Spirit to enable me to live a life of miracles. Help me to stay in touch with You, so that Your wonder-working power can flow through me to the world around me. In Jesus' name, amen.

Endnote

1. E.M. Bounds, *Answered Prayer* (New Kensington, PA: Whitaker House, 1994), 111.

CHAPTER FOURTEEN

The Wonders of God's Peace

Prayer is the place to draw from the peace of God.

I understand those who ask themselves: What good is life? What does it all mean? What do you do when all you have worked for is gone and you are in the middle of nowhere? I know what such doubts feel like because that is exactly where I was shortly after I left Nigeria and wound up in Togo. I originally intended to go to Europe, but I had problems obtaining a visa. An acquaintance from Togo told me it would be simple to get a visa to enter Europe from there. Once I landed, things proved tougher than I imagined. Nothing seemed to be working out as I had planned.

Originally, I had visions of expanding my business to other nations. It was a multifaceted operation that started with industrial washing—cleaning industrial plants, cafes, theaters, and other facilities. From there I branched out into interior decorating and handling general merchandise. In addition to this full-time endeavor, I was actively involved in ministry. The youth coordinator at our church, I was also involved in the prayer ministry and other activities.

It was the latter that proved a sticking point in my life. Though I had set my sights on growing my business, in reality I was a modern-day Jonah, running from God's call on my life. I knew He wanted me to preach and teach others His Word, but I didn't want to devote all my efforts to His Church. Ultimately, I wound up selling the business and living off the proceeds. After arriving in Togo, I found all doors closed for obtaining a visa. Worry became my constant companion. I found myself fasting often, but more as a symbol of desperation than to seek God's direction.

Finally, I found myself stranded, with no money, nowhere to go, and no idea what to do. All I had was my suitcase with a few belongings, a Bible, and some books I had brought from Nigeria. I slept on someone's floor at night and would awake in the morning with blood on my body where the mosquitoes had dive-bombed me during the night. I even had trouble communicating with most people since I couldn't speak the dominant language, French. Helpless, I resorted to prayer and visiting different churches. One day at a church, a woman I had never met before asked, "Brother, do you know you are called?" This happened three times in three different places, but each time I brushed it off with remarks like, "Everyone's called."

Still, I kept praying. After several weeks I sensed a breakthrough. God's peace surrounded me, reassuring me that everything would be all right, no matter how bad things appeared at the moment. The more I prayed, the more peace I felt. One day I heard the Holy Spirit say, "I'm calling you. This is my plan for you." Soon after that, because of the awesome peace I felt, I became increasingly confident and bold in talking to others about Christ. As people saw God's presence in my life, they came to me to tell me about their problems. When

I prayed with them, they saw breakthroughs in their lives and started blessing me financially.

I also saw God perform miracle after miracle. One woman who had diabetes was healed. Another one who had been infertile became pregnant. After I prayed with a man who wanted to go to London for business, he got his visa. Others who needed blessings in their business received them. Despite these blessings, satan didn't stop his attacks. Reminding me of the bleak circumstances I faced, he whispered things like, "You've followed God from your youth and now He has abandoned you." In response, I kept praying. The circumstances didn't change immediately, but in spite of that I felt an incredible peace. I now knew the truth that God was my Provider, Protector, and King. As long as I followed Him, I would be safe.

Peace that Passes Understanding

Thanks to experiences like that, I have come to understand that when I spent time in earnest prayer, problems don't instantly vanish. I have lived through some challenging, perplexing difficulties in life and ministry, and not just in Togo. More than once it has looked as if the world was caving in on me. Yet because of these struggles, I have learned lasting lessons about trusting God and receiving His uncommon peace, which transcends all understanding. Trust is the basis for this unmovable peace in the midst of difficulties. Prayer enables me to bear difficulties with peace intact, opening my eyes to God's hand at work. Sensing Him in the situation gives me assurance and the determination to persevere.

While trouble belongs to the present state of humanity, it is nothing new: *"Man who is born of woman is of few days and full of trouble"* (Job 14:1 NKJV). Though a praying saint, Job endured a heap of troubles. Yet in the midst of them, he never turned his back against God and he maintained a strong faith.

His secret came from prayer, which gave him the ability to draw from God's peace. Because of prayerlessness, those with weak faith—who know nothing of God's disciplinary processes in dealing with His people—often turn their backs on Him and take foolish steps when troubles come.

How much better, wiser, and greater our peace when we take everything to God. If you go to your prayer closet, it is possible to experience overflowing peace no matter what the trial. As we journey through life, we must be prepared to face obstacles. Those who view life through the prism of eternal sunshine and expect only ease and pleasure are pursuing a false image. The murmurings, complaints, and rebellion of Christians facing troubles are vain and silly. They need to read again about the children of Israel in the wilderness and remember Moses' admonition as they neared the end of the journey:

> *Remember how the Lord your God has led you in the desert for these forty years, taking away your pride and testing you, because He wanted to know what was in your heart. He wanted to know if you would obey His commands* (Deuteronomy 8:2).

The Peaceful Heart

In the last chapter I discussed miracles and the role of prayer in their release. The other key to releasing God's miraculous power is a peaceful heart, like the kind Moses demonstrated when leading Israel to freedom:

> *And Moses said to the people, "Do not be afraid. Stand still, and see the salvation of the Lord, which He will accomplish for you today. For the Egyptians whom you see today, you shall see again no more forever. The Lord will fight for you, and you shall hold your peace"* (Exodus 14:13-14 NKJV).

For God to fight for Israel, the people simply needed to hold their peace. The supernatural intervention of God's miracles cannot be realized through a people with restless hearts. Troubled hearts cannot experience God's power; without peace you cannot exercise God's authority. Only a heart of prayer can become a heart of peace because prayer keeps your relationship with God close, creating a way for peace to flow continuously to your heart.

Peace is only possible through Jesus, a truth Paul pointed out in his letter to the Romans: *"Therefore being justified by faith, we have peace with God through our Lord Jesus Christ"* (Rom. 5:1 KJV). Peace is not merely a state of calmness and ease, which many people seek in troubled times. It is ultimately the condition that can exist between God and humans, based on the redeeming work of Christ.

The introduction of sin into the perfect world God created brought separation between God and man. Adam and Eve's choice to disobey God in the Garden of Eden created an obstacle between the Creator and His creation. It destroyed the hope of a divine relationship between God and people. Sin ruined the harmony that had existed between God and humanity; only the death of the Son of God could restore it. Christ's death on the cross—the weight of mankind's sin, past, present, and future, resting on Jesus' shoulders—paid the penalty for all transgressions. The massive temple veil dividing the holy place from the Holy of Holies split in two from top to bottom, signifying reconciliation between people and God (see 2 Cor. 5:18-19).

Jesus' death restored the possibility of peace with God. However, only when a person bows at His pierced feet in a prayer of repentance and receives forgiveness will peace with God become a reality. Prayer plays a vital role in possessing this perfect harmony with God and bringing the sinner into God's peace (see Rom. 10:8-13). However, there is another kind of peace that prayer delivers to the hearts of those who pray, as expressed by Paul in his letter to the Philippians.

The Peace of God

Be anxious for nothing, but in everything by prayer and supplication, with thanksgiving, let your requests be made known to God; and the peace of God, which surpasses all understanding, will guard your hearts and minds through Christ Jesus (Philippians 4:6-7 NKJV).

There is a difference between having "peace with God" (see Rom. 5:1) and knowing the "peace of God" mentioned in Philippians 4:7. The first has to do with coming into harmony with God at the point of salvation. The latter flows into your heart when you are walking in obedience to Him. The peace of God is a single light within your heart, proving that you are in the center of His will.

In both cases, prayer is where you take hold of this peace. Prayer helps people make peace with God and secures divine guidance amid the anxieties and cares of this world. Until you have peace with God, you cannot experience the peace of God. Paul's letter to the Philippians was specifically to the believers at Philippi. He was not writing to unbelievers. Scholars believe that Paul wrote this letter while he was in prison.

Paul understood feeling overwhelmed. Without a doubt Paul experienced stress during his imprisonment. Yet during that time, he wrote, *"Rejoice in the Lord always. Again I will say, rejoice"* (Phil. 4:4 NKJV). As an apostle of prayer, Paul's prayer life paved the way for him to experience "the peace of God," even in prison. The reason for his peaceful heart despite his difficulties was the knowledge that he was in the center of God's will.

Avoiding Anxiety

Cares are a prevalent plague of humanity, coming in all shapes, at all times, and from a variety of sources. They are universal in their reach, touching everyone regardless of age, circumstance, or social status. Doubt, fear, unbelief, and anxiety are the natural result of sin, which robs people of the peace of God. There are the cares of the home, the cares of business, the cares of occupation, the cares of survival, the cares of poverty, and its opposite—the cares of riches. Only through prayer can we escape these cares.

We live in an anxious world. Since we are surrounded by cares, how can we live among them and keep God's peace in our hearts? Paul's caution to the Philippians in 4:6-7, which I quoted above, is the divine remedy. Following Paul's advice will enable you to overcome anxiety and live free from worldly cares. To avoid getting enslaved in worry and fretting, we must avoid anxiety.

Anxious implies being pulled in different directions and distracted, disturbed, and annoyed. Jesus warned against this in His Sermon on the Mount in Matthew 5–7. He told the crowd, *"So don't worry about tomorrow, because tomorrow will have its own worries..."* (Matt. 6:34). Christ endeavored to show people the secret of a peaceful mind freed from unnecessary cares about food, clothing, and shelter. Paul echoed this instruction. Cares divide, distract, and destroy unity and calm.

In his letter to the Philippians, Paul shows the need to guard against cares and offers a secret to overcoming them—which is prayer. It is the way to quiet every distraction, hush every anxiety, and lift every care from an enslaved mind. Only prayer can relieve unnecessary burdens and save us from worrying over things that we cannot control. The peace of God, that tranquil state that assures you that you are in God's will and drives away fear, is a peace that transcends life's cares. The peace that comes from God will guard your heart and mind in Christ. The "and" that connects the main instructions of Philippians 4:6-7 shows a connection between prayers of thanksgiving and the peace of God that can flow into the hearts and minds of those who pray.

In a world where cares, temptations, and countless concerns bombard us, how is it possible to live in the peace of God? We do it by retreating daily to our prayer closets, where we learn to cast our cares upon God and exchange them for His peace. A heart that knows how to pray is a heart constantly in touch with God, drawing from His peace. Prayer will turn your focus to the heavenly realm, where no distractions, fears, doubts, or worries exist. Nothing causes God to worry or fret. Once you turn your attention to Heaven in prayer, your heart links to the never-ending flow of His peace. This is why Paul wrote to the Colossians, *"Set your mind on things above, not on things on the earth"* (Col. 3:2 NKJV).

Prayer helps you to set your heart toward Heaven. We need to engage constantly in the School of Prayer. A lifestyle of prayer will yield the secrets of a happy life, one filled with perfect peace that comes only from God.

Problems, Prayer, and Peace

There is a connection between problems, prayer, and God's peace. We cannot appreciate prayer and the peace of God until we find ourselves in a sticky situation that is beyond our natural ability to resolve. The psalmist Asaph promised when speaking of God, *"Call upon Me in the day of trouble; I will deliver you, and you shall glorify Me"* (Ps. 50:15 NKJV).

Prayer is the most appropriate thing for a person in the time of trouble because prayer recognizes God in the midst of the situation. It sees God's hand and seeks His deliverance, which brings peace. While perplexing problems may not be pleasant, they reveal our helplessness and disclose our weakness. Yet, anyone who knows how to turn to God in such times will be blessed. If God stands above the trouble, the most sensible step is to take the problem to Him in prayer.

Christ's disciples knew about the link between problems, prayer, and drawing from the peace of God. They considered every problem as an opportunity to engage God in earnest prayer in order to secure His peace. The record in Acts 4 is a good example. One passage says:

> *After Peter and John left the meeting of leaders, they went to their own group and told them everything the leading priests and the elders had said to them. When the believers heard this, they prayed to God together, "Lord, you are the One who made the sky, the earth, the sea, and everything in them"* (Acts 4:23-24).

Later they continued,

> *And now, Lord, listen to their threats. Lord, help us, your servants, to speak Your word without fear* (Acts 4:29).

The chapter concludes,

> *After they had prayed, the place where they were meeting was shaken. They were all filled with the Holy Spirit, and they spoke God's word without fear* (Acts 4:31).

It is natural and reasonable for oppressed, broken, and bruised souls to bow low at the footstool of mercy and seek God's face. During their greatest time of persecution by the enemies of the Gospel, the early disciples turned to God. Their prayers stirred a refilling of the Holy Spirit, which empowered them with boldness. Though their persecutors intended to rob them of their peace, the disciples reaffirmed their connection with God through prayer, which helped them speak His Word with boldness. Nowhere will a troubled soul more likely find peace than in the prayer closet. Take heart in David's declaration:

> *The Lord hears good people when they cry out to Him, and He saves them from all their troubles. The Lord is close to the brokenhearted, and He saves those whose spirits have been crushed* (Psalm 34:17-18).

Prayer magnifies the presence and peace of God in the time of problems. The troubles are what make God sweet, giving new life to prayer and bringing you closer to the feet of Jesus. Because we live in a fallen world, we must always be prepared to receive God's disciplinary dealings. No matter what He is trying to teach us or how He is trying to mold us, we can experience His peace in prayer. Prayerless people are sadly disappointed and surprised when trouble breaks into their lives. Their weakness in prayer becomes an obstacle to reaching out to draw from God's peace. If they only knew that through prayer we can conquer every opposing force and claim victories over our arch enemy. When prayer becomes your chief weapon, you are destined to stay at peace in a troubled world.

Peace Is Possible

As Jesus prepared for His imminent death, He offered these words of comfort to His disciples: *"I leave You peace; My peace I give you. I do not give it to you as the world does. So don't let your hearts be troubled or afraid"* (John 14:27). His message on peace established a reason to hope for generations of His followers to come. It remains a signal to us today in a world of conflict and unrest.

Billions are craving peace. Nations seek it through countless methods. People from every language are looking for it as well.

Some think if they make *just a little more* money, they will secure peace of mind. Yet the avenues that people engage in to find peace fall short. The peace that comes from the world system is only temporary security, with no lasting foundation. Like the stock market "wealth" that disappeared by the trillions in 2008 and 2009, it may be here today and gone tomorrow.

Perfect peace is found in a person, Jesus, the Prince of Peace (as Isaiah 9:6 calls Him). Christ gives peace to everyone connected to Him by a living relationship founded on prayer and obedience to His Word. Through this prayer connection we experience an unshakeable peace that comes from God's presence, even in a troubled world. *"You will keep him in perfect peace, whose mind is stayed on You, because he trusts in You"* (Isa. 26:3 NKJV).

Peace is possible even in your greatest difficulty, whether it is the loss of a job, the sudden death of a loved one, the loss of a financial investment, or the dissolving of a long-standing marriage because of death or divorce. Where your mind is focused and where your trust is anchored determines the possibility of peace in tough times. God commits to give us His peace when we place our trust in Him. When we anchor our trust in God, the enemy cannot win. God will use such occasions to increase our spiritual maturity and demonstrate that He is the sustaining power in our lives.

How then do we possess such trust, which is a stronger word for faith? It comes from a closer relationship with God, which develops a steady, committed, and diligent flow of belief. These qualities bring you to the place where your relationship with Him gives you the confidence to trust and obey Him, no matter what circumstances life throws into your path.

A prayerless Christian who only visits God when difficult times strike can never develop this level of trust. Your prayer life determines how much peace you experience. When you practice being in God's presence through constant fellowship with Him, you will experience a continuous flow of peace. A troubled heart is a heart not trusting solely in God. Follow David's advice: *"Trust in the Lord, and do good; dwell in the land, and feed on His faithfulness"* (Ps. 37:3 NKJV).

How can you expect to trust God and feed on His faithfulness when you have no prayer life? Prayer is a divine arrangement, designed for the benefit of men and women. You use it to prove His faithfulness. God is faithful to keep His promise of giving you peace even in your most difficult times, but you will never know His depth until you learn to trust in Him and put prayer to the test in your darkest hour. Earnest prayer channels God's revealed peace into your heart.

Christ Is Our Peace

Christ Himself is our peace. He made both Jewish people and those who are not Jews one people. They were separated as if there were a wall between them, but Christ broke down that wall of hate by giving His own body. The Jewish law had many commands and rules, but Christ ended that law. His purpose was to make the two groups of people become one new people in Him and in this way make peace (Ephesians 2:14-15).

The countless millions who are turning the world upside down searching for peace don't realize genuine peace is not of this world. Success and fame can never guarantee it. Money can't buy it. Since genuine peace does not depend on outward circumstances, it is possible to experience inner serenity beyond comprehension. If you will bring your struggles and needs to the foot of the cross, you will find an overflowing source of peace.

A heart at rest is not rooted in some worldly principle or philosophy. It can only be realized through an intimate relationship with the person of Jesus Christ. He broke down the wall of separation between us and His Father. Through Christ's resurrection, He abolished this enmity. Because of Him, you have access at any time to draw from the never drying fountain of peace in Heaven. *"It is through Christ we all have the right to come to the Father in one Spirit"* (Eph. 2:18).

The devil may try to distract you by drawing your attention away from Christ to things that seem important at the time. I encourage you not to waste your life looking for peace in the wrong places. Make a serious commitment to develop a relationship with Christ through diligent prayer. Your prayer life keeps Heaven open for a steady flow of God's peace. Prayerlessness keeps Heaven closed and blocks the free flow of God's peace. Rise up from unbearable burdens and storm the gates of Heaven with your prayers. You will see the Heavens open and rain down peace.

Pray this prayer:

Lord, my peace comes from the knowledge that You are in control. When the enemy strikes and adversity comes, help me to stay in prayer with confidence that my peace will not be taken away because You are my peace. In Jesus' name, amen.

CHAPTER FIFTEEN

The Wonders of an Open Heaven

Prayer is the major route to an open Heaven.

I will never forget the Sunday in 2004 that I took the microphone at a church in Italy and the Holy Spirit said, "Today I want to heal people." Those words reverberated like a command through my mind, colliding with my intention—and desire—to preach a message titled "Let God be God." Now the Spirit was challenging me. Was I willing to let God be God and put aside my plans for His? When I hesitated, the Spirit said, "Call the people out who need help, who don't have 20-20 eyesight. Those who need to wear glasses at work. Those who use contacts. Call them out. I want to heal them right now."

When I obeyed, the atmosphere buzzed with electricity. With faith released to do its work, some people jumped up and down at their seats while others flooded into the aisles. A few excited souls tossed their eyeglasses on the altar. When they did, I told them, "Don't come and take them back later. They are defiled now. They won't work. You are healed!" In response, people clapped, danced, shouted, and praised God for His amazing power. After nearly three weeks in Italy, this would be my last Sunday at this church. This time of healing and celebration went on so long it also marked my shortest sermon of this visit.

Before I left later in the week, I heard numerous stories about what had happened that day. One woman told of wearing glasses for more than 22 years, but no longer needing them. Another woman told her friends, "I can drive my car without glasses now. When the man of God spoke, I dropped my glasses. When I went home without them and my daughter asked why I wasn't wearing them, I said, 'Because I have 20-20 vision now.'" This woman worked in a canning plant, a detail-oriented job that required glasses to be able to keep up with production lines. When her co-workers asked why she wasn't wearing glasses, she told them. The devil whispered that she should be wearing glasses, but she stood fast. When she came to Bible study on Wednesday night, she still wasn't wearing her glasses.

This rather mind-boggling experience demonstrates the joy of living under an open Heaven. It is uncovering the third Heaven—the home of God's throne—for the access of believers on earth. Paul saw this in a powerful vision, which he wrote about in Second Corinthians 12, where he described an encounter so profound he didn't know whether it occurred inside or out of his body. In this process, a believer's deliberate involvement in passionate prayer removes every blockage and obstacle in the heavenlies.

An open Heaven also uncovers the Heavens for the release of angelic traffic (God's messengers) to earth. The story of Jacob in Genesis 28:1-22 attests to this connection. God's intention is to bring His moral government to earth, which is only possible under an open Heaven. This is something we should all crave, as shown by Isaiah's plea: *"Oh, that You would rend the heavens! That You would come down! That the mountains might shake at Your presence"* (Isa. 64:1 NKJV). It is also how Jesus taught

His disciples to pray: *"Your kingdom come. Your will be done on earth as it is in heaven"* (Matt. 6:10 NKJV).

We must see an open Heaven for the Kingdom of God to come and His will to be done on earth. However, this means spiritual warfare. As Ephesians 6:12 warns, every believer faces principalities, powers, rulers of the darkness of this world, and spiritual wickedness in high places. These satanic agents' primary mission is to oppose and attempt to stop every move of God on the earth.

To triumph over demonic spirits, we must pray. According to Luke 3:21, prayer is one of the most effective instruments to open Heaven. This is the primary reason satan opposes and resists believers' prayers. The devil understands prayer's impact and its power to bring Heaven's influence to earth. He knows that once Heaven opens over an area, he loses his control over that area. When that happens, God exposes the power of sin and breaks the devil's hold. Acts 8:1-13 outlines how Philip went to Samaria to preach the Gospel and the power of God overtook the city because Philip entered it with the influence of Heaven.

Open Heart to Open Heaven

Satan doesn't want Heaven's influence on earth, so he releases fiery darts to block saints' prayers or to attempt to weaken them and cause them to lose their desire to pray. The devil knows a believer under an open Heaven is more likely to establish the Kingdom of God on earth. The believer under a closed Heaven is powerless. As an example of our prayer goal, we can look to Daniel, the remarkable saint who blasted open the Heavens over Babylon. His prayer life paved the way for the divine awareness of the fear of God in that godless place.

After some cunning governors who were jealous of Daniel's authority persuaded the king to make it illegal to pray—a pretext for getting Daniel thrown in the lions' den—the prophet withstood the attack. Darius was so impressed he wrote a letter to all people, nations, and languages that said,

> *I am making a new law for people in every part of my kingdom. All of you must fear and respect the God of Daniel. Daniel's God is the living God; He lives forever. His kingdom will never be destroyed, and His rule will never end* (Daniel 6:26).

What a powerful decree! Don't take the amazing nature of this letter for granted. Because Daniel introduced the influence of God's Kingdom through his commitment to prayer, it paralyzed the satanic influence over Babylon during the reign of King Darius. This shows that Heaven decides the activities on earth, not the powers of this world. The prayers of righteous men and women give Heaven permission to determine the outcome.

However, until people open up their hearts in prayer, there can be no open Heaven. Proverbs 20:27 calls the human spirit the candle of the Lord; Heaven only opens because people's hearts are opened to accommodate God. The more a believer opens up his or her heart to God, the more the Heavens open over these believers. The measure of your openness to God will determine the measure of His openness to you. The prayer that opens Heaven is one that comes from an open heart. Any believer who wants to see Heaven open must be willing to pray.

The prayer that influences Heaven flows out of a pure heart. A heart filled with insincere and impure motives can never get Heaven's attention. Heaven only responds to the cry of a desperate person: *"The sacrifices of God are a broken spirit, a broken and a contrite heart; these, O God, You will not despise"* (Ps. 51:17 NKJV). Not until your prayer reflects the energy of a contrite heart can it influence God to open the Heavens over your life.

Closed Heavens

If there is such a thing as an open Heaven, it follows that there is also a closed Heaven. This is one of the curses listed in Deuteronomy 28:23, *"The sky above will be like bronze, and the ground below will be like iron"*. A similar curse is recorded in Leviticus 26:19: *"I will break your great pride, and I will make the sky like iron and the earth like bronze"*. When the Heavens over you become brass, it is impossible for God's blessings to reach you. Daniel had to fast for 21 days to open Heaven. When his angel of blessing arrived, he said,

> *Daniel, do not be afraid. Some time ago you decided to get understanding and to humble yourself before your God. Since that time God has listened to you, and I have come because of your prayers. But the prince of Persia has been fighting against me for twenty-one days. Then Michael, one of the most important angels, came to help me, because I had been left there with the king of Persia* (Daniel 10:12-13).

This story illustrates how Heaven can close over a believer. In Daniel's case, satanic obstacles blocked him, but he persevered in prayer until the answer came. The tenacity of Daniel's prayer caused Heaven to open, releasing a stronger angel to contend with the prince of persia. If prayer lacks a stirring of the soul, there will be no mighty movement toward God. Feeble prayer has no tenacity and inner power to open a closed Heaven. Under an open Heaven, God's blessings keep coming. When Heaven closes, you can labor in prayer and never experience a harvest.

When Heaven Opens

1. Revelation Comes

Any time Heaven opens over your life, you possess the ability to see beyond the natural:

- When heaven opened over the prophet Ezekiel, he had a divine vision. *"It was the thirtieth year, on the fifth day of the fourth month of our captivity. I was by the Kebar River among the people who had been carried away as captives. The sky opened, and I saw visions of God"* (Ezek. 1:1).

- Isaiah also received a revelation of God's glory when Heaven opened: *"In the year that King Uzziah died, I saw the Lord sitting on a throne, high and lifted up, and the train of His robe filled the temple"* (Isa. 6:1 NKJV).

- Paul experienced a supernatural vision during his open Heaven: *"Now it happened, when I returned to Jerusalem and was praying in the temple, that I was in a trance and saw Him [Jesus] saying to me, 'Make haste and get out of Jerusalem quickly, for they will not receive your testimony concerning Me'"* (Acts 22:17-18 NKJV).

- Job was another notable saint who received an open Heaven of revelation, the primary reason he was blessed beyond measure. The record of Job's experience is found in Job 29:1-25.

2. The Rain of Blessings Falls

Heaven must open for the rain of blessings to come to earth.

The Lord will open up His heavenly storehouse so that the skies send rain on your land at the right time, and He will bless everything you do. You will lend to other nations, but you will not need to borrow from them (Deuteronomy 28:12).

Every blessing you experience will stem from an open Heaven. Rain comes to make the things planted on earth grow:

"Then Elijah prayed again, and the rain came down from the sky, and the land produced crops again" (James 5:18).

Rain can also represent the anointing of the Holy Spirit. An open Heaven releases God's anointing on your life. Every form of dryness around you becomes wet with this blessing. This rain causes every seed of the word you speak to produce fruit. Without rain you will never experience a harvest. Just as the rain makes the seed grow, the anointing makes things work. When you are soaked with the rain of God's anointing, obstacles become miracles and barriers become breakthroughs. In order to accomplish an extraordinary impact that will bring glory to God, we must stay under an open Heaven. It affects every area of those living under this cloud. These rains bring peace, joy, prosperity, and divine protection—things that make life colorful.

How wonderful it would be if all believers could position themselves to live under an open Heaven. It would make a world of difference. Living this way is a must if you want to touch your generation with the reality of the Kingdom of God and the proof of His power. Prayer is a key to unlocking Heaven over your life.

Benefits of an Open Heaven

1. People Will Seek You Out

When you live this way, you become someone others want to know. The influence of Heaven on your life attracts people to you. Jesus had this influence, which put Him in the position of becoming a wanted man. He held the answers to people's questions.

> *Immediately, as Jesus was coming up out of the water, He saw heaven open. The Holy Spirit came down on*

Him like a dove...When they found Him, they said, "Everyone is looking for You" (Mark 1:10,37).

2. You Will Carry God's Anointing

When you operate under an open Heaven, the anointing is not a feeling, but a force that comes over you. Jesus carried God's anointing, which is why He provided solutions to every human problem He encountered. Acts 10:38 and Luke 4:14 relate how God gave Christ the Holy Spirit and power and how He went everywhere, doing good and healing those who were oppressed by the devil.

3. You Will Have Divine Protection

Living under an open Heaven keeps you under divine protection. When the Lord covers you with His feathers, you will stay under the Almighty's shadow. The psalmist promised,

> *He who dwells in the secret place of the Most High shall abide under the shadow of the Almighty...You shall not be afraid of the terror by night, nor of the arrow that flies by day, nor of the pestilence that walks in darkness, nor of the destruction that lays waste at noonday* (Psalm 91:1;5-6 NKJV).

4. You Will Live in the Realm of Possibility

Another benefit of an open Heaven is that it brings you into the realm of possibility, where all things are possible because you trust in God. Just as all things are possible with God (see Luke 1:37), all things are possible to the person who believes (see Mark 9:23). All things were possible to Jesus because of Heaven's influence in His life.

5. You Will Have Access to Divine Insights

As I established earlier, an open Heaven brings revelation. This revelation enables you to experience breakthroughs and enjoy God's supernatural blessings. Examples of saints who received revelations from Heaven and a breakthrough in their lives include:

- Peter, who learned that God's grace was for all (see Acts 10:9-11).

- John, who saw Heaven (see Rev. 4:1).

- Isaiah, who saw God (see Isa. 6:1).

- Jacob, who received supernatural direction (see Gen. 31:9-13).

Saints Under an Open Heaven

Every extraordinary person in the Bible who made an impact started his or her journey with God with an open Heaven experience, borne out of their prayer life. The perfect example is Jesus, the Son of God. He came from Heaven to fulfill the mission of redemption of humanity. But before He embarked on this divine mission, He needed an open Heaven over His ministry:

> *When all the people were being baptized by John, Jesus also was baptized. While Jesus was praying, heaven opened and the Holy Spirit came down on him in the form of a dove. Then a voice came from heaven, saying, "You are my Son, whom I love, and I am very pleased with you"* (Luke 3:21-22).

Jesus did not enter into full-time ministry until He blasted open Heaven over His life. With this unique experience, He embarked on a 40-day fast while praying for greater empowerment to accomplish His mission. Afterward, satan tempted Him, but Jesus defeated the enemy. Prayer played a major role in Jesus opening Heaven and keeping it open. It is impossible for the devil to defeat you when you engage Heaven through fervent prayer.

Every extraordinary work recorded in Christ's ministry came because Jesus operated in divine power and provision. He brought the influence of God's government to earth, made possible by a faithful life of prayer. Jesus understood that He came to a lost world. Above Him, His Father watched, willing and able to rescue people. Jesus knew He had to build the bridge linking Heaven and earth through the instrument of prayer, which opened Heaven and made it possible for God to reach men and women. Because of how He lived, Jesus charged His disciples to never spread the Gospel until they received a touch from Heaven (see Acts 1:4-8).

Other Examples

Daniel

A captive in Babylon, Daniel's unusual prayer life tore open Heaven. His commitment to intense prayer paved the way for Heaven to influence this nation and further God's moral government. Most notably, when the king ordered everyone to not ask anything of God or any other king for 30 days—or face being cast into the lions' den—Daniel paid no attention. Daniel 6:10 describes how he continued to thank God three times a day as he always had. This should be the practice of everyone who wants to be used by God. Nothing could dissuade Daniel from prayer, even though it resulted in him being thrown into the lions' den. Thanks to an open Heaven, God sent an angel into the den and shut the lions' mouths so they didn't touch a hair on his head.

The book of Daniel is full of records of angelic visitations because his prayer life opened the way for divine activity in a heathen place. Such a man of faith will always stand out among people in his generation. Daniel was a striking example of a young man who feared God and resolved to remain faithful to Him, regardless of the cost. No wonder he ended up providing remarkable evidence of how prayer brings down Heaven to earth.

Jacob

Jacob enjoyed a unique experience with God. Prior to the all-night prayer session where he encountered the Lord, he wasn't an outstanding example of righteousness. Still, he believed in the God of prayer and called on Him when he faced trouble. Jacob left home and headed for the home of Laban, his uncle, because he feared his brother, Esau, would take revenge on him for stealing his birthright. As night fell, he stopped at a certain place to refresh himself. As he slept, he had a colorful dream in which he saw the angels of God ascending and descending on a ladder that stretched from earth to Heaven.

When Jacob awakened, he exclaimed, *"Surely the Lord is in this place, but I did not know it"* (Gen. 28:16). After this, Jacob made a covenant with God in which he vowed that if God remained with him and protected him and provided him food and clothing, he would follow Him and treat the place where he slept as God's house, where he would give a tenth of his earnings (see Gen. 28:20-22).

Through his vow Jacob conditioned the rest of his life for protection, blessing, and divine guidance. Not surprisingly, Jacob flourished in the house of Laban, marrying two of Laban's daughters and fathering a dozen children. He also increased in wealth. The influence of Heaven over Jacob's life put him in position to receive multiple blessings, including the creation of the nation of Israel. This man Jacob made prayer a lifetime companion, which continuously opened Heaven.

Solomon

Solomon cannot be left out of an account of people who experienced an open Heaven through prayer. Whatever may have happened later in life because of Solomon's mistakes, at the beginning of his reign this king prayed regularly. One example is when he went to Gibeon to offer sacrifices. While there, the Lord appeared to him in a dream and said, *"Ask for whatever you want Me to give you"* (1 Kings 3:5). This encounter formed Solomon's character. His request to God was steeped in humility; he began by comparing himself to a child. He also noted his status as God's servant in the midst of His people, too numerous to be counted. To help him with the task of governing them, Solomon asked for an understanding heart and discernment (see 1 Kings 3:7,9).

Solomon's request pleased God. He didn't ask for long life, riches, or the lives of his enemies. At the dedication of the temple Solomon prayed a remarkable prayer; prayer was the foundation of God's house. The Heavens opened at the end of his comprehensive, pointed, intense intercession. God clearly heard it: *"When Solomon finished praying, fire came down from the sky and burned up the burnt offering and the sacrifices. The Lord's glory filled the Temple"* (2 Chron. 7:1).

Elijah

Elijah, the praying prophet, is another notable saint. His Mount Carmel contest with the prophets of Baal (see 1 Kings 18) in the face of a backslidden nation—with a faithless king—is a notable exhibition of faith and prayer. In this contest, the prophets of Baal failed. No fire from Heaven fell in answer to their frantic cries. With confident assurance, Elijah called fire down from Heaven and Israel back to God. This demonstration was rooted in the personal knowledge of the role of righteous prayer in bringing Heaven's moral government to earth.

Verses 36-39 tell the story:

> *At the time for the evening sacrifice, the prophet Elijah went near the altar. "Lord, You are the God*

of Abraham, Isaac, and Israel," he prayed. "Prove that You are the God of Israel and that I am Your servant. Show these people that You commanded me to do all these things. Lord, answer my prayer so these people will know that You, Lord, are God and that You will change their minds." Then fire from the Lord came down and burned the sacrifice, the wood, the stones, and the ground around the altar. It also dried up the water in the ditch. When all the people saw this, they fell down to the ground, crying, "The Lord is God! The Lord is God" (1 Kings 18:36-39).

Elijah was a prophet of prayer with direct access to God. Likewise, men or women with a solid relationship with God can command an open Heaven. Prayer deals with the One who controls Heaven and earth. Elijah's prayer aimed to determine the existence of God; the Lord's visible answer settled the question. The Heavens remain still and emotionless when we fail to pray and stir up divine activity to influence events on earth. Elijah acted according to what God had said. Yet, even after Israel turned back to God, no rain fell. Elijah did not fold his arms and say, "The promise has failed." Instead, he prayed, using the key to open Heaven for rain. The outcome of his prayer is clear evidence that persistent prayer commands Heaven's attention.

Charles G. Finney

A great revivalist, Finney's passion spurred him to agonizing prayer as he cried for cities to be revived. His earnest prayer brought him into an open Heaven ministry. His prayers paved the way for the Holy Ghost to bring conviction and repentance to people even before he reached the places hosting his meetings. Finney brought down the influence of Heaven and took entire cities for God. Today's generation needs people who will labor in prayer until the Heavens open over their nations.

Travailing Prayer

Travailing prayer is the kind that goes beyond the power of the flesh. It loses its focus on time, tiredness, and public opinion. If you want to know what it looks like, visit a labor ward in a hospital and watch women travailing to give birth to children. Initially, agony covers their faces. Travailing prayer looks the same. Taking cities for God requires effort. You don't slide up a hill; you climb it by working against the pull of gravity. If you want to come down, you simply sit down and let go. You can slide down with ease.

You must separate yourself from worldly concerns to concentrate on prayer long enough to generate strong desire. That demands considerable energy. Every experience of an open Heaven recorded in the history of revivals has come through the hands of strong, passionate, prayer-filled people. Their prayers are like bombs in the Spirit that break apart the darkness and satan's strongholds over people, cities, and nations.

Charles Finney prayed in a way that his prayer shaped his character. It revolutionized his life and others. His prayers made a lasting mark on Church history and altered the events of his era. The wonders of an open Heaven can be a reality in the twenty-first century if we will cultivate a life of prayer and purity of heart.

Pray this prayer:

Heavenly Father, I recognize that Your move on earth is affected by my prayer. You have shown me that it is persistent prayer that opens Heaven for the rain of Your blessings to fall. Today I receive grace to pray like Elijah for an open Heaven over my life. In Jesus' name, amen.

CHAPTER SIXTEEN

The Wonders of Purity

Prayer is the lung through which purity breathes.

Our church's prayer meeting was just wrapping up when a young businessman stepped into the building, asking if he could talk to me. Felix told me, "Brother, I have a problem." I asked him about the nature of his problem, but he couldn't force himself to reveal the details. Three times he repeated, "Brother, I have a problem." Finally, hoping to encourage him, I said, "Listen, I won't expose this to anybody, but I need to know what's wrong. What is your problem? Tell me so I can help you."

Finally, after hanging his head for a while longer, he asked, "How can a Christian live in the spirit of fornication? How can I even call myself a Christian? I had sex with a woman before I came to church. Each time I do this it troubles my spirit. I can't continue going this way. One of my strongest temptations is my daughter's landlord. She's the one I had sex with right before I came. How can you help me to break this thing?"

I was living in Togo at that time, I knew what a strong battle this man had ahead of him. A strong spirit of sexual immorality hung over this West African nation; adultery and fornication were an accepted way of life. Many of the inhabitants engaged in voodoo, and women often wandered the streets half-dressed, trying to appease some strange god. It was a modern reminder of the city of Ephesus, where the people worshiped all kinds of gods and Christ's followers struggled with constant temptations to immorality. Anyone trying to conquer this spirit on their own faced an uphill battle.

Although we prayed, I encouraged him to come to my home later so we could talk further. Before that appointment, the Holy Spirit directed me to have him read the seventh chapter of Romans, where Paul discusses the enormous struggle he faced with his flesh, asking the question, "Who will deliver me from this body of death?" As we concluded our counseling session, I told him, "Go home tonight and the Holy Spirit is going to visit you. God will wake you up at midnight and the Spirit of God is going to touch you. When you wake up, read Romans 7. You will have victory over this sin."

We prayed before he left. The next day he returned to ask, "What did you do to me? I woke up at midnight and read the passage you gave me and I broke into tears. I tried to contain myself so I wouldn't wake my neighbor, but I couldn't stop. It was like somebody was beating me. I cried aloud all the way through Romans 7, until I reached verse 24. After a time of weeping and crying, around one or two in the morning it felt like a heavy weight had lifted off my shoulders. I felt like I had been cleansed of that spirit of sexual immorality."

We stayed in touch for the next several years. Each time we talked, this businessman told me he still had victory over that sexual spirit. He had seen firsthand how prayer can bring Christ's followers to a state of purity, which is a matter of the heart. Your ability to see God's power manifested in your life depends on the condition of your heart. It takes pureness of heart to connect to Him. Prayer is the avenue by which your heart receives holy cleansing and links you to the Holy Spirit, Jesus' blood, and the Word of God. These enable you to overcome satanic forces of filthiness and defilement.

In Old Testament times, Ezekiel prophesied that this was exactly what God would do for Israel:

> *Then I will sprinkle clean water on you, and you will be clean. I will cleanse you from all your uncleanness and your idols. Also, I will teach you to respect Me completely, and I will put a new way of thinking inside you. I will take out the stubborn hearts of stone from your bodies, and I will give you obedient hearts of flesh. I will put My Spirit inside you and help you live by My rules and carefully obey My laws. You will live in the land I gave to your ancestors, and you will be My people, and I will be your God. So I will save you from all your uncleanness. I will command the grain to come and grow; I will not allow a time of hunger to hurt you* (Ezekiel 36:25-29).

This passage shows that purity is an act of God. He sprinkles the clean water of His Word on us to cleanse us. He puts His spirit within us, causing us to keep His ways and follow His Word. However, God only does this when we engage Him in prayer. God will only bring what He said to pass after you have inquired of Him. The longer you stay in your prayer closet, the more you receive God's cleansing of your heart and renewal of your spirit.

The Holy Ghost and Purity

The Holy Ghost is a reliable help in conflict with the sin and filthiness that come to pollute your heart. Jesus called the Spirit the Comforter and declared His mission on earth.

> *Nevertheless I tell you the truth; it is expedient*
> *for you that I go away: for if I go not away, the*
> *Comforter will not come unto you; but if I depart, I*
> *will send Him unto you. And when He is come, He*
> *will reprove the world of sin, and of righteousness,*
> *and of judgment* (John 16:7-8 KJV).

In prayer, the Holy Spirit reveals the sin in our hearts. He convicts us and stirs us to confess to the Lord. Then we receive forgiveness, restoring a pure heart.

This is an ongoing process, but only those committed to prayer can stay pure before God. It is impossible to live a life of purity without the Holy Ghost's help. John the Baptist introduced Him as the one to come after Jesus:

> *He will come ready to clean the grain, separating the*
> *good grain from the chaff. He will put the good part*
> *of the grain into His barn, but He will burn the chaff*
> *with a fire that cannot be put out* (Matthew 3:12).

You need the Holy Spirit to purge your heart. Malachi says He is like a refiner's fire:

> *But who can endure the day of His coming? And who*
> *can stand when He appears? For He is like a refiner's*
> *fire and like launderer's soap. He will sit as a refiner*
> *and a purifier of silver; He will purify the sons of*
> *Levi, and purge them as gold and silver, that they*
> *may offer to the Lord an offering in righteousness*
> (Malachi 3:2-3 NKJV).

The Holy Ghost's refining nature comes to purify you each time you pray.

The disciples' prayer in the upper room invited the Holy Ghost to come on the day of Pentecost:

> *When the day of Pentecost came, they were all together in one place. Suddenly a noise like a strong, blowing wind came from heaven and filled the whole house where they were sitting. They saw something like flames of fire that were separated and stood over each person there* (Acts 2:1-3).

Spiritual fire came down from Heaven to purge the disciples, purifying them to carry the holy oil of Heaven that impacted their world. Prayer served as the pipeline for this purifying fire. Is defilement or sin in your life robbing you of God's power? It may be anger, malice, fear, lying, or immorality. Without any feeling of shame or failure, go boldly to God, acknowledge your problem, and ask for His help. Tell Him, "Lord, I need Your help in this area of my life. I tried on my own, but can't overcome this sin. Send your Holy Spirit fire to purge this area of my life." If you pray this prayer, I am confident that you will see victory over that sin.

Confession Brings Purity

The condition of your heart in prayer is vital. It must be kept clean from contamination and unconfessed sin. If your heart is contaminated, it becomes impossible for God to reach you. Every heavenly blessing is communicated to your heart before it reaches the outer world. A contaminated heart will block God's blessings. Isaiah addressed this reality when he wrote,

> *Behold, the Lord's hand is not shortened, that it cannot save; nor His ear heavy, that it cannot hear. But your iniquities have separated you from your God; and your sins have hidden His face from you, so that He will not hear* (Isaiah 59:1-2 NKJV).

Iniquities are root sins that come through your family bloodline. They flow from one generation to another and can hinder you from reaching God. But in prayer, the powerful cleansing agent of Christ's covenant blood can purge iniquities. However, you must apply it through prayers of faith to receive forgiveness and purify yourself. Follow the advice of John, who wrote,

> *But if we walk in the light as He is in the light, we have fellowship with one another, and the blood of Jesus Christ His Son cleanses us from all sin. If we say that we have no sin, we deceive ourselves, and the truth is not in us. If we confess our sins, He is faithful and just to forgive us our sins and to cleanse us from all unrighteousness* (1 John 1:7-9 NKJV).

When you confess sin that the Holy Spirit reveals, it breaks the power behind it because you have exposed it to the truth of God's Word. Sins only have the power to defile you when they remain hidden. Confession plays a powerful role in your life. You receive the conviction of the Holy Ghost about the sin in your heart. Then with your mouth you confess that sin to receive freedom:

> *We believe with our hearts, and so we are made right with God. And we declare with our mouths that we believe, and so we are saved* (Romans 10:10).

Verbal confession also releases the burdens of your heart and brings them into agreement with God. And it releases His mercy, obtaining forgiveness from sins that pollute your heart. Until we uncover our sins through confession, we remain in an impoverished state: *"He who covers his sins will not prosper, but whoever confesses and forsakes them will have mercy"* (Prov. 28:13 NKJV). Unconfessed sins are one of the leading reasons many believers are not experiencing God's blessings.

Although unconfessed sins pose an obstacle between you and God, there are great blessings attached to a pure heart. The Roman emperor and Stoic philosopher Marcus Aurelius—often known as "the wise one"—once said, "The one thing worth living for is to keep one's soul pure."[1] Souls pure before God stand ready to be used by Him to touch their generation. Even before David became king, God chose him to lead Israel because He saw the pureness of his heart:

> *After God took him away, God made David their king. God said about him: "I have found in David son of Jesse the kind of man I want. He will do all I want him to do"* (Acts 13:22).

God testified that David was a man after His heart because he had a pure heart. The Lord sees the heart while humans look at outward appearances. His pureness of heart kept God near to David, who served his generation by keeping God's will (see Acts 13:36). David secured this pureness by committing himself to the School of Prayer. He regularly confessed his weakness and sin to God and depended on the Spirit's guidance throughout his life.

We need to learn from David's example. Confession kept his heart free from contamination, even when he fell to temptation with Bathsheba. There were many occasions in David's life when he could have chosen to allow his heart to be polluted by sin, but he resisted. When he slipped, he confessed it and repented. Read Psalm 51, which contains David's plaintive cry after Nathan confronted him over his sin with Bathsheba.

Purity and Holiness

A heart of purity produces a life of holiness. These only come through a commitment to prayer and obedience to God's Word. In the Sermon on the Mount, Jesus said, *"Blessed are the pure in heart: for they shall see God"* (Matt. 5:8 KJV). This means that purity of heart puts you in position to see God manifest Himself in your life. Wise Solomon once wrote, *"Whoever loves pure thoughts and kind words will have even the king as a friend"* (Prov. 22:11). This Scripture shows how purity of heart brings us to the place where even high officials become our friends—including God, the King of kings.

While purity is the condition of our hearts, holiness means that we avoid sin and obey God. Prayer is the lungs through which holiness and purity breathe—a life-giving force that causes them to become reality. Prayer is the essential ingredient in forming God's character in you. When you talk to God, you rub minds and spirits with Him and the blood of Christ purifies you. I often experience God's nature whenever I spend quality time in prayer. There is always a freshness and relief that comes to my heart, giving me strength to live boldly for Him.

The disciples experienced this as well. Their prayer gave them a fresh filling of the Holy Spirit, which instilled boldness to speak. Prayer purified their hearts and infused them with God's character. If they had not prayed, their hearts would have been contaminated by fear. Your soul will be renewed in the place of prayer, too. New strength enters your soul and spirit whenever you kneel.

Men and women who accomplish more for God are people whose souls and spirits are renewed. Prayer provides the energy that keeps God near and helps you walk in righteousness. Lack of purity and holiness in the Body of Christ has caused a power shortage in many churches. It takes purity to see God's anointing flow. As Solomon wrote, *"Let your garments always be white, and let your head lack no oil"* (Eccl. 9:8 NKJV). The white garment represents purity. The divine anointing that lifts burdens will fall on you when you maintain a life of righteousness and holiness.

Righteousness is what you are—it is God's gift to you. Holiness is what you do—it is your gift to God. Holiness is making sure you maintain a righteous stand with God, staying away from the things that defile and contaminate your relationship with Him. The Psalmist put it this way: *"I have restrained my feet from every evil way, that I may keep Your word"* (Ps. 119:101 NKJV). Such action keeps the holy oil of God fresh upon your life.

Prayer is the channel that releases these qualities. It kept grace in David's life:

> *Who can understand his errors? Cleanse me from secret faults. Keep back Your servant also from presumptuous sins; let them not have dominion over me. Then I shall be blameless, and I shall be innocent of great transgression. Let the words of my mouth and the meditation of my heart be acceptable in Your sight, O Lord, my strength and my Redeemer* (Psalm 19:12-14 NKJV).

Prayer is also the channel by which purity, holiness, and righteousness flow. But if purity is blocked by sin and a passive attitude toward prayer, it becomes impossible to live a holy, pure life. The character of God develops in us each time we come before Him in brokenness. He reveals His nature to us and replaces our weaknesses with His strength. This is an ongoing process. As we learn to pray and spend quality time in His presence, He changes us into His likeness (see 2 Cor. 3:18). He purges sin from us and manifests His image through us.

Purity Guarantees Answered Prayer

Nothing brings speedy answers to prayer like pureness of heart. The prayers of righteous men and women produce results, as evidenced by James' instruction: *"Confess your sins to each other and pray for each other so God can heal you. When a believing person prays, great things happen"* (James 5:16).

Righteous behavior gives you authority in prayer before the throne of Heaven, where you draw power to work in God's Kingdom.

The importance of righteousness can't be overstated. The Psalmist pointed out, *"Your throne, O God, is forever and ever; a scepter of righteousness is the scepter of Your kingdom"* (Ps. 45:6 NKJV). Only the prayer of a righteous person can command the righteous scepter of God's Kingdom to release answers. Many prayers have gone unanswered, which may indicate they failed to come from a righteous heart—which is necessary to follow the command to come boldly before God: *"Let us therefore come boldly to the throne of grace, that we may obtain mercy and find grace to help in time of need"* (Heb. 4:16 NKJV).

Because righteousness produces boldness (see Prov. 28:1), a pure heart can boldly approach God's throne. Jesus prayed effectively and powerfully because He lived a sin-free life, which gave Him authority. Only pure, righteous prayers can attract Heaven's attention. Christ's God-likeness caused His prayers to be heard and answered; *"Who, in the days of His flesh, when He had offered up prayers and supplications, with vehement cries and tears to Him who was able to save Him from death, and was heard because of His godly fear"* (Heb. 5:7 NKJV). Answered prayer marks an exchange with Heaven, showing the realization of a relationship with God.

Purity Establishes Signs and Wonders

Even though every believer has the ability to walk in signs and wonders, it takes purity of heart to produce them.

> But God's strong foundation continues to stand. These words are written on the seal: "The Lord knows those who belong to Him," and "Everyone who wants to belong to the Lord must stop doing wrong."...All who make themselves clean from evil will be used for

> *special purposes. They will be made holy, useful to the Master, ready to do any good work* (2 Timothy 2:19,21).

The vessel who operates in signs and wonders must first be purged to possess purity.

We see a clear picture of this in the time of Elisha. Gehazi, his servant, was destined to obtain a double portion of his master's anointing, but he lost it. When Elisha gave Gehazi the rod to raise the Shunammite woman's dead son in Second Kings 4, the rod would not produce because Gehazi's heart was full of corruption. This became evident when he pursued Naaman, seeking a talent of silver and two changes of garments. If Gehazi couldn't produce miracles, neither can anyone else with a corrupt heart. It is impossible to manifest signs and wonders until you deal with your corruption.

Your heart is the point of connection where God's power flows through you. Until you do away with sin, signs and wonders can't follow you. Purity of heart allows you to walk in accordance with the Word of God and enables you to manifest signs and wonders. Jesus pointed out: *"He who has My commandments and keeps them, it is he who loves Me. And he who loves Me will be loved by My Father, and I will love him and manifest Myself to him"* (John 14:21 NKJV).

Consider that Scripture and note the phrase, *"I will manifest Myself to him."* In other words, Jesus was saying, "I will bring him to the realm of signs and wonders, a realm of supernatural manifestations." The condition to walk in these supernatural manifestations is for you to keep this commandment of purity. Jesus lived in purity. No one could convict Him of sin (see John 8:46).

As a result, He walked in signs and wonders.

Purity Is Your Choice

To walk in purity, you must take a deliberate step to avoid every form of defilement. Daniel lived in purity and became a vessel of honor in God's hands because he remained pure amid idol worship.

> *But Daniel purposed in his heart that he would not defile himself with the portion of the king's delicacies, nor with the wine which he drank; therefore he requested of the chief of the eunuchs that he might not defile himself. Now God had brought Daniel into the favor and goodwill of the chief of the eunuchs* (Daniel 1:8-9 NKJV).

Daniel's choice to live without defilement paved the way for him to become a vessel of honor. God did not make that choice; it was Daniel's responsibility. Likewise, we must choose a life of purity and holiness to become useful to the Master: *"Therefore if anyone cleanses himself from the latter, he will be a vessel for honor, sanctified and useful for the Master, prepared for every good work"* (2 Tim. 2:21 NKJV). The word *if* in this Scripture makes it clear that you determine what kind of vessel you will be.

With holiness, the power of sin no longer has dominion over you, even though you still live in a sinful world. Because we live in a world of sin, we all have many temptations to face. Yet you have the inner power to say "no" to choices that defile you. God has put within you the willpower to say "no" or "yes" to every temptation. Daniel kept his vessel clean; so can you. Many believers fail to walk in purity because they don't want to accept responsibility for their choices. They conduct their lives in a manner that gives sin free access, and they excuse their poor choices by saying, "God knows my heart."

In order to walk in purity before God, you must choose to depart from every unclean thing, which is anything that defiles your heart and makes it unfit to communicate God's power. It takes personal effort, backed up by God's grace, to avoid sin. The power of choice cannot be underestimated; it is a vital force against the influence of evil.

> *Look, today I offer you life and success, death and destruction....Today I ask heaven and earth to be witnesses. I am offering you life or death, blessings or curses. Now, choose life! Then you and your children may live* (Deuteronomy 30:15,19).

God has set a standard for us to live in purity, but He has given you a choice. Take the time to examine yourself and see if you are involved in any evil. Sin hinders you from experiencing and walking in God's favor. Every great man and woman recorded in biblical history took the responsibility to walk in godliness. These men and women understood that it required an effort. It is an exercise:

> *But do not follow foolish stories that disagree with God's truth, but train yourself to serve God. Training your body helps you in some ways, but serving God helps you in every way by bringing you blessings in this life and in the future life, too* (1 Timothy 4:7-8).

If you don't take steps to say "no" to temptation, you will never have victory over sin and cannot walk in purity. Here are some steps to enforce your will against sin:

1. Magnify the gain of godliness in your mind above the momentary pleasures of sin (see Heb. 11:25-26).

2. Submit yourself to God in prayer, asking Him for the grace to overcome the temptation (see James 4:7).

3. Just as you resist the devil by submitting to God, you can say no to sin by submitting yourself to God in prayer (see Luke 22:40).

4. Pray continuously. Prayer is your greatest weapon, turning promises into reality and helping you make the choice to remain pure.

Pray this prayer:

Holy and righteous God, I come to You today. Search my heart and see if there is anything that displeases You. Cleanse my heart from secret faults. Keep me from presumptuous sins and don't allow them to rule my life. Help me to overcome satanic forces of filthiness and defilement so I can walk in purity of heart before You. In Jesus' name, amen.

Endnote

1. Marcus Aurelius, quotation found at Famous Quotes and Authors, http://www.famousquotesandauthors. com/authors/marcus_aurelius_quotes.html, (accessed April 14, 2010).

CHAPTER SEVENTEEN

The Wonders of God's Promises

Prayer turns God's promises into reality.

In 2002, my good friend Rotimi had a startling experience while using the restroom. As he was about to flush the commode, he happened to look down and notice the presence of blood. It gushed so heavily that it shocked him. Did it indicate cancer? Some other dreaded disease? Although this happened two or three times a day that week, he didn't say anything about it to friends or family members. Instead, he reviewed the thousands of promises in the Bible, including Isaiah 53:5, which says that by Christ's wounds—some translations call it "stripes"—we are healed.

That Sunday, Rotimi went to the altar at his church in Baltimore. Kneeling, he straightened one hand toward Heaven and prayed: "Jesus, about two thousand years ago You died on the cross and paid for my healing. Your Word proclaims that by Your stripes I have been healed. Today I have come to receive my healing. Thank you. In Jesus' name, I receive it."

Afterward, he went home and still didn't tell anyone about his problem, not even his family doctor. The next day when he went to the bathroom, blood remained. The next day nothing changed. All week nothing changed—until the seventh day after he had prayed. Suddenly, the blood had vanished, as quickly as water would stop flowing when you turn off a faucet. He did not experience a single trickle of blood that day, nor any day since.

Rotimi never felt concern that God wouldn't heal him. "I had a strong confidence that I was going to be healed the day I prayed," he told me. "So I never worried about it."

That isn't the end of the story. In the summer of 2009 he met a woman on a visit to Ohio whose husband was in the hospital. Suddenly he felt prompted by the Holy Spirit to share about the miraculous experience he had had seven years earlier. When he did, the woman broke into tears. When she stopped crying, she said, "God sent you to me. What you went through is the same thing my husband is going through now." She desperately needed the assurance that God not only knew about her husband's situation, but was capable of doing something about it.

Fulfillment Brings Joy

The fulfillment of God's promises in our lives brings a joy beyond words. Scripture encourages us to follow Him; those who do with faith and patience will inherit His promises. Consistent prayer nurtures faith and patience, but you won't develop these qualities if you are out of fellowship with God. One shining example is Abraham (originally Abram), a man whose lifestyle of prayer was the foundational principle that brought the promises of God into reality. Although faith and patience played a role in fulfilling them, prayer gave voice to his faith and patience:

> *But Abram said, "Lord God, what can You give me?*
> *I have no son, so my slave Eliezer from Damascus*
> *will get everything I own after I die." Abram said,*
> *"Look, You have given me no son, so a slave born*
> *in my house will inherit everything I have." Then*
> *the Lord spoke His word to Abram: "He will not be*
> *the one to inherit what you have. You will have a*
> *son of your own who will inherit what you have."*
> *Then God led Abram outside and said, "Look at the*
> *sky. There are so many stars you cannot count them.*
> *Your descendants also will be too many to count."*
> *Abram believed the Lord. And the Lord accepted*
> *Abram's faith, and that faith made him right with*
> *God* (Genesis 15:2-6).

Abraham voiced his faith by asking, "What can You give me?" Fourteen years after Ishmael's birth (patience), the promise of a son with Sarah became a visible reality with the birth of Isaac. There are many believers who confess *"exceedingly great and precious promises"* that Peter described in Second Peter 1:4 (NKJV), but lack any tangible, concrete evidence of them. This is because they fail to engage God in prayers of faith. They fail to understand the role prayer plays in making these promises precious and practical.

You should possess a deep insight of the promises of God for your life while positioning yourself in prayer for their fulfillment. It is possible to have a powerful, specific promise from God and not see its fulfillment. Without prayer, it remains voiceless. God gave us promises to inspire and energize us to pray. The prayer of faith gives a promise realization and an earthly location. There are two reasons for this:

- God has circumscribed Himself to the laws of prayer: *"Ask, and God will give to you. Search, and you will find. Knock, and the door will open for you. Yes, everyone who asks will receive. Everyone who searches will find. And everyone who knocks will have the door opened"* (Matt. 7:7-8).

- Satan can create invisible hindrances around a promise: *"We wanted to come to you. I, Paul, tried to come more than once, but Satan stopped us"* (1 Thess. 2:18). The devil tries to hinder God's promises from being fulfilled because he knows that for every realization, the Lord is glorified: *"If you remain in Me and follow My teachings, you can ask anything you want, and it will be given to you. You should produce much fruit and show that you are My followers, which brings glory to My Father"* (John 15:7-8).

Prayerless hearts will never see the fulfillment of God's promises. These are things pertaining to life and godliness, body and soul, and time and eternity. No matter how exceedingly great and precious God's promises are, until you vocalize them in prayer, they will not become a reality. God has given us such promises as: *"Now we hope for the blessings God has for His children. These blessings, which cannot be destroyed or be spoiled or lose their beauty, are kept in heaven for you"* (1 Pet. 1:4). Still, it is our responsibility to ask Him to fulfill them in our lives: *"Thus says the Lord, the Holy One of Israel, and his Maker: 'Ask Me of things to come concerning My sons; and concerning the work of My hands, you command Me"* (Isa. 45:11 NKJV).

To help you get a stronger grasp of the promises God has given to His people, I am devoting the rest of this chapter to biblical promises and their realization through prayer. Note that God's promises and fulfillment link directly with asking. God's promises that manifest in our lives are directly proportionate to prayer investments.

Abraham's Promise

Earlier, I quoted from a passage from the first part of Genesis 15. This conversation between Abraham (then known as Abram) and God resumed later:

> *Then the Lord said to Abram, "You can be sure that your descendants will be strangers and travel in a land they don't own. The people there will make them slaves and be cruel to them for four hundred years. But I will punish the nation where they are slaves. Then your descendants will leave that land, taking great wealth with them"* (Genesis 15:13-14).

This promise to Abraham and his descendents included:

- His seed would be servants in a strange land for 400 years.

- They would face affliction.

- Afterward, God would judge their captors.

- Abraham's people would leave the nation with great substance.

Though God did not name the nation where Abram's descendents would be strangers, He later reveals that it is Egypt. God's promise lay dim and voiceless for longer than He originally declared because of a lack of prayer. Though God made a promise, it came overdue because there was no channel by which it could flow; the fulfillment took 430 years. The desperate cry of the children of Israel got Heaven's attention and the Lord sent Moses to deliver Israel:

> *After a long time, the king of Egypt died. The people of Israel groaned, because they were forced to work very hard. When they cried for help, God heard*

them. God heard their cries, and He remembered the agreement he had made with Abraham, Isaac, and Jacob. He saw the troubles of the people of Israel, and He was concerned about them....The Lord said, "I have seen the troubles My people have suffered in Egypt, and I have heard their cries when the Egyptian slave masters hurt them. I am concerned about their pain, and I have come down to save them from the Egyptians. I will bring them out of that land and lead them to a good land with lots of room—a fertile land. It is the land of the Canaanites, Hittites, Amorites, Perizzites, Hivites, and Jebusites. I have heard the cries of the people of Israel, and I have seen the way the Egyptians have made life hard for them. So now I am sending you to the king of Egypt. Go! Bring My people, the Israelites, out of Egypt" (Exodus 2:23-25; 3:7-10).

The channel of prayer by which this promise could have been realized earlier was blocked because Israel's prayerlessness posed an invincible obstacle. Yet when they cried out to God, He delivered in a big way:

The Lord caused the Egyptians to think well of them, and the Egyptians gave the people everything they asked for. So the Israelites took rich gifts from them....on the very day the four hundred thirty years ended, the Lord's divisions of people left Egypt (Exodus 12:36,41).

With the fulfillment of this promise, God's name was sanctified and glorified in Egypt and surrounding nations. Likewise, fulfilled promises in your life bring Him glory. However, if you are unwilling to engage God in prayer, it will hinder the realization of His promises and deny Him glory. Their fulfillment is like a spring of love, demonstrating your willingness to yield your time to spend time with Him: *"I love the Lord, because He has heard my voice and my supplications. Because He has inclined His ear to me, therefore I will call upon Him as long as I live"* (Ps. 116:1-2 NKJV).

These actions, prayers, and the realization of God's promises become like a bottomless spring that wells up, further inspiring us and motivating us to stay near to God. Conversely, nothing will harden the heart and blind us to the invisible, eternal Spirit as much as unfulfilled promises caused by prayerlessness. *Earnest prayer takes hold of God's promises and induces Him to do what He has promised.* For example, the Lord instructed me to sow a sacrificial seed of $1,000 during a Christian convention. So, I prayerfully meditated on a specific promise of God concerning giving (see Gen. 26:12). I then obeyed God's command and gave it cheerfully. Nothing happened immediately, and I kept reminding God what he told me. Through my daily prayers, within ten days God blessed me with contribution to my ministry of $25,000 that was unsolicited. This is only one example of how "Prayer Works" in turning promises into reality.

More Promises to Abraham

The angel of the Lord called to Abraham from heaven a second time and said, "The Lord says, 'Because you did not keep back your son, your only son, from Me, I make you this promise by My own name: I will surely bless you and give you many descendants. They will be as many as the stars in the sky and the sand on the seashore, and they will capture the cities of their enemies. Through your descendants all the nations on the earth will be blessed, because you obeyed Me'" (Genesis 22:15-18).

This was a clear promise to Abraham. He exhibited deep trust when he willingly offered to sacrifice his only son, Isaac. His extraordinary act of faith moved God to seal the promise with an oath. Hebrews 6 describes how God, because He could call on no one greater, swore by Himself to bless Abraham and multiply his descendants. This strong, powerful promise was irrevocable. Yet, the vessel through whom it was to flow was Rebekah, Isaac's wife. Her barren womb posed a roadblock. However, Isaac did not fold his arms waiting for God to act. He took the responsibility to pray: *"Now Isaac pleaded with the Lord for his wife, because she was barren; and the Lord granted his plea, and Rebekah his wife conceived"* (Gen. 25:21 NKJV).

The word *pleaded* can also mean "prayed." Isaac's heartfelt prayer opened the roadblock, creating an expressway for the fulfillment of the promise. Without the force of prayer, God's promise—no matter how powerful and irrevocable—could have been hindered. The role of prayer in turning God's promises into reality cannot be underestimated. Nothing on earth can overcome the force of fervent prayers. The energy of prayer is required in the simplest challenges or the most complex. *Without prayer, God's promises for your life can remain unfulfilled.*

Are your prayers producing fruit? Prayer takes hold of a promise and conducts it to its glorious end. It removes satanic obstacles and creates a path toward fulfillment. Your persistent prayer of faith puts God to work. I have often mentioned the prophet, Daniel, in this book because he is such a sparkling example of someone who activated God through persistent prayer. He knocked down every satanic resistance to secure answers.

If your prayers are feeble and weak, they will have no power to execute God's purposes. No matter how strong and powerful a promise, if it lacks prayer it may lack fulfillment. According to Hebrews 6:17-18, God is bound to His promises.

For this reason, there are no limitations, adverse conditions, weaknesses, or inabilities that can or will hinder the realization of His promise—if we fulfill the conditions of prayer.

From Jeremiah to Daniel

Speaking to Israel on God's behalf, Jeremiah outlined the timeframe of their captivity and prophesied its ending. This precise message illustrates how a promise waits on prayer:

> *This is what the Lord says: "Babylon will be powerful for seventy years. After that time I will come to you, and I will keep My promise to bring you back to Jerusalem. I say this because I know what I am planning for you," says the Lord. "I have good plans for you, not plans to hurt you. I will give you hope and a good future. Then you will call My name. You will come to Me and pray to Me, and I will listen to you. You will search for Me. And when you search for Me with all your heart, you will find Me"* (Jeremiah 29:10-13).

This passage shows how the promise of Israel being taken captive, then released, hinged on prayer: *"You will come to Me and pray to Me, and I will listen to you."* God was saying, "You are going to be in captivity for 70 years in Babylon, and at the end of that time, I will fulfill My promise by bringing you back to your land. But this will only happen when you engage Me in prayer." God recognized prayer as the required instrument.

If we trace this message through other books, we can see how this promise was fulfilled in Daniel's time:

> *During Darius' first year as king, I, Daniel, was reading the Scriptures. I saw that the Lord told Jeremiah that Jerusalem would be empty ruins for seventy years. Then I turned to the Lord God and*

> *prayed and asked Him for help. To show my sadness,*
> *I fasted, put on rough cloth, and sat in ashes* (Daniel
> 9:2-3).

Daniel was among the Israelites carried away as captives to Babylon. As a man of prayer, he understood the time for the end of captivity. So, he positioned himself to seek God in order to see the promise take place. Though God told Jeremiah about it, it took Daniel's prayer to break the chains. Promise and prayer are an inseparable combination that helps manifest God's plans. Do you have a promise from God? I dare you to go to Him in prayer in the same manner as Daniel and Elijah. I am confident that you will see the promise become a living reality.

New Testament Fulfillment

Though Isaiah lived seven centuries before Christ's coming, he spoke more than once about the Savior who would set people free. He told the people, *"The Lord Himself will give you a sign: The virgin will be pregnant. She will have a son, and she will name Him Immanuel"* (Isa. 7:14). This wonderful promise, which would bring the salvation of humanity, found its realization in the New Testament. Still, prayer was required to see this redemptive promise come to pass.

We find the earthly vessels of prayer for its fulfillment in two committed vessels, Simeon and Anna (their stories appear in Luke 2 and 3). The prayers of these two saints paved the way for the coming of the Messiah. Simeon had such an intense desire to see the promise fulfilled that the Holy Spirit revealed that he would not die until he saw Christ's birth. Simeon drew deep assurance from this promise. Likewise, the prophetess Anna prayed in the temple where Jesus was dedicated to God's service. Like those of Simeon, her prayers and fasting helped created a highway for the Savior's coming.

It is reasonable to believe that the prayers of these two committed prayer vessels opened the Heavens for angelic visitations to Zacharias and Elizabeth, the parents of John the Baptist, and Joseph and Mary, Christ's earthly parents. The promise of God is the basis, inspiration, and heart of prayer. Not only do His promises inspire us to pray, but they also assure us of specific answers.

The Promise of the Spirit

Jesus declared the promise of the Holy Spirit to His disciples before He ascended to Heaven. However, He included a condition for its fulfillment:

> *And being assembled together with them, He commanded them not to depart from Jerusalem, but to wait for the Promise of the Father, "which," He said, "you have heard from Me; for John truly baptized with water, but you shall be baptized with the Holy Spirit not many days from now"* (Acts 1:4-5 NKJV).

The powerful promise that empowered the disciples to be effective witnesses for Christ came, but only after nearly two weeks of unified, persistent prayer. Jesus had already told them, *"I will send you what My Father has promised, but you must stay in Jerusalem until you have received that power from heaven"* (Luke 24:49). While many of us are prone to take action, the disciples' instruction was to wait in Jerusalem. Acts makes it clear that while they waited, they prayed: *"They all continued praying together with some women, including Mary the mother of Jesus, and Jesus' brothers"* (Acts 1:14). And while they prayed, the Holy Spirit fell on them, they were filled with the Holy Ghost, and they spoke in other tongues at the Spirit's direction (see Acts 2:4).

The inducement of power came in the place of earnest, expectant prayer. If it took this kind of dedication for the disciples to see the fulfillment of this promise, it will take the same kind of praying today. The Lord is still willing to fill His people with the power of the Holy Spirit, a promise that will be realized by asking in faith: *"...How much more your heavenly Father will give the Holy Spirit to those who ask Him"* (Luke 11:13).

The Promise of Divine Presence

Before Christ left the earth, He promised: *"...I will be with you always, even until the end of this age"* (Matt. 28:20). This promise of divine presence gave the disciples assurance that He heard their prayers. They rested on the promise each time they were in trouble. Peter's supernatural release from prison, recorded in Acts 12:1-17, depended on the disciples' prayers. When the saints put prayer to the test, they saw Christ's promise of divine presence fulfilled. God sent an angel from Heaven to deliver Peter. If the disciples had not prayed, God wouldn't have dispatched an angel and Peter's life and earthly ministry would have ended like that of James, who died at the hands of Herod (see Acts 12:2).

Prayer Creates Promises

Prayer not only turns promises to reality, it creates promises and brings them to reality. As long as prayer has an audience with God, it is capable of creating promises. The Scripture is filled with stories of men and women of prayer who did this. One example is Elijah. Though God gave the prophet the promise of rain (see 1 Kings 18:1), He didn't give him the promise of fire (see 1 Kings 18:38). Elijah's prayer created the latter. God sent fire from Heaven to consume the burnt sacrifice because the promise Elijah created was in unison with God's will, even though it was not part of His spoken promise.

Another example is Queen Esther. She didn't have a direct promise from God that He would deliver her from the king's decree, which could have proved fatal to the Jews. Still, she fasted and prayed and, contrary to the nation's law, went to see the king. God granted her favor with the king and delivered the Jews. Her faith, prayer, and three-day fast created the promise and brought the realization.

Though Daniel had no specific promise that God would make known the king's dream to him, he and his associates prayed, which brought revelation and interpretation. Daniel's prayer and that of his associates obtained and created the promise for the fulfillment. The record of this event appears in Daniel 2:14-19.

King Hezekiah is another figure who had no promise that God would heal him of the sickness that threatened his life. The word of the Lord came to him through the mouth of a prophet that he would die. Still, he prayed in faith and asked God to change his future, a fascinating story of miraculous intervention that you can find in Isaiah 38:1-6. Likewise, God's rich and refreshing promises can be fulfilled in your life, if only you surrender yourself to Him in prayer.

Pray this prayer:

Dear Lord, You have shown me from this book that without prayer, Your promises for my life will remain inactive. Help me to give voice to every specific and general promise You have declared concerning my life. I will no longer wait and watch for Your promises, but will pray in faith for their fulfillment. In Jesus' name, amen.

CHAPTER EIGHTEEN

The Wonders of Divine Surrender

Prayer is the crying expression of our dependence on God.

For many people, the word *surrender* conjures up images of conflict and overpowering forces that should be avoided at all costs. In worldly terms, surrender carries the connotations of giving in and giving up to a dreaded enemy. Yet for the follower of Christ, surrender represents a pleasant, peaceful experience. Biblical surrender to God is to be admired and pursued. The Christian life starts with submitting to Jesus' lordship and following His leadership through prayer. When we do, affliction, adversity, and conflict shrink before God's superiority.

I saw the truth of this statement in the winter of 2008, during a profound breakthrough involving my younger brother and his wife. An unseen problem with unforgiveness—which was revealed by the Holy Spirit during prayer—had blocked numerous prayers on their behalf. When she surrendered her "rights" and submitted to God's way, she saw Him intervene in her situation with dramatic, life-changing action.

This situation began when my brother called from Nigeria to update me on his wife's situation. When I asked about her pending delivery, he replied, "Please pray. She is past due. Before I called, we spent four days praying for her after they admitted her to the hospital. This is a Christian facility. All the doctors and nurses on staff are born-again believers. They've been praying for her to deliver the baby, too, but we haven't seen any breakthrough. She has had labor pains for several days without any sign of delivery. The doctors cannot find any possible reason in the natural for this."

After he finished describing her condition, we prayed. I released my faith, reminding God of His promise to heal. When we finished, I asked him to call again and let me know the outcome. The next day, nothing had changed. As he talked, I waited silently, asking the Holy Spirit to let me know why all these prayers had not been answered. Immediately the Spirit impressed on me the reason: my brother's wife was holding unforgiveness toward our mother and younger sister. For this reason, our prayers for her could not be answered.

I immediately shared this divine revelation and suggested that my brother return to the hospital. I told him to call me again so I could confront his wife with this reality and ask her to confess the sin of unforgiveness. Two hours later my brother called from his wife's bedside, then handed the phone to her. Though I spoke with her gently, I clearly described the impression the Holy Spirit had laid on my heart.

"Yes, you are right," she said quietly when I finished. "I am guilty of unforgiveness."

After we finished talking, I asked my brother to anoint her with oil. Then I agreed with them in prayer that their baby would be delivered safely. The next day, my brother called again.

"This time, it's good news!" he said, laughing. "She delivered our baby at midnight, after we had prayed."

God still answers prayer when we surrender to Him, whether it is the spirit of unforgiveness, self-centeredness, or some other human shortcoming. *Effective prayer is the mark of total surrender of all that is in us, yet it brings every possession that He has for us.*

Willing Submission

Romans 10:9-10 demonstrates the willing submission we must embrace if we are to follow Christ:

> *If you declare with your mouth, "Jesus is Lord," and if you believe in your heart that God raised Jesus from the dead, you will be saved. We believe with our hearts, and so we are made right with God. And we declare with our mouths that we believe, and so we are saved.*

Your verbal confession is an expression of faith, showing the role of prayer in surrendering to Christ. Vocalizing saving faith in Jesus indicates submission to God's plan of salvation.

Verse 13 adds, *"Anyone who calls on the Lord will be saved,"* making it evident that salvation is a combination of faith and confession. Faith that lies silent in your heart without a vocal expression will never guarantee salvation. The Bible illustrates this further with the examples of Zacchaeus (see Luke 19), Bartimaeus (see Mark 10), and one of the thieves crucified with Christ (see Luke 23).

In each of these examples, the individual cried out an expression of faith—an indication of dependence on God—before Jesus could endorse their salvation.

Zacchaeus vocalized his faith as the evidence of genuine conviction of repentance: *"But Zacchaeus stood and said to the Lord, 'I will give half of my possessions to the poor. And if I have cheated anyone, I will pay back four times more'"* (Luke 19:8). Immediately after this heart-moving confession, Jesus said, *"Salvation has come to this house today, because this man also belongs to the family of Abraham"* (Luke 19:9). Zacchaeus' confession, a form of prayer, presented the evidence that he had surrendered his life to the lordship of Christ.

A close look at the story of blind Bartimaeus also reveals a combination of faith and prayer. His expression of total dependence on God brought about his miracle:

> *As Jesus was leaving there with His followers and a great many people, a blind beggar named Bartimaeus son of Timaeus was sitting by the road. When he heard that Jesus from Nazareth was walking by, he began to shout, "Jesus, Son of David, have mercy on me!" Many people warned the blind man to be quiet, but he shouted even more, "Son of David, have mercy on me!" Jesus stopped and said, "Tell the man to come here." So they called the blind man, saying, "Cheer up! Get to your feet. Jesus is calling you."... Jesus asked him, "What do you want Me to do for you?" The blind man answered, "Teacher, I want to see." Jesus said, "Go, you are healed because you believed." At once the man could see, and he followed Jesus on the road* (Mark 10:46-49,51-52).

Wonders happen when we yield ourselves to God as an act of divine surrender. We can trust in His unlimited power to save and deliver us from anything that is beyond our ability to overcome. Just as Bartimaeus pushed against all visible obstacles that were trying to stop the release of his faith, God expects us to cry out through prayer and voice our dependence on Him.

The thief on the cross (see Luke 23:39-43) expressed his dependence on Jesus to receive eternal life when he said, *"Jesus, remember me when You come into Your kingdom"* (Luke 23:42). This statement of faith starkly contrasted with the other criminal, who earlier had taunted Him, saying that if He was the Christ He should save Himself and both of them. Jesus responded to the second man's faith with the promise, *"I tell you the truth, today you will be with Me in paradise"* (Luke 23:43).

The condemned thief recognized that he was a sinner worthy of death, acknowledged the lordship of Christ, and surrendered to His saving grace. By these simple steps of faith, in the twinkling of an eye he was translated from certain, lasting death to eternal life in Heaven.

Our Ultimate Source

Mark 9:23 says, *"...All things are possible for the one who believes."* Likewise, all things are possible to believers who pray because faith in God and prayer are deep expressions of dependence on Him. Though faith may be silenced because it is of the heart, prayer is an expression of faith that is never silenced. Prayer is often asking God for something that you do not have, that you desire, and that you know God has promised to give to you as an answer to prayer.

Prayer's importance cannot be overemphasized as an act of submission to God's plans and purposes. Genuine, heart-linked prayer is also a sign of loyalty to God's will. His will covers three major areas of life—body, soul, and spirit. As Third John 2 says, *"Beloved, I pray that in all respects you may prosper and be in good health, just as your soul prospers"* (NASB). As a loving, caring heavenly Father, God's gracious desire is to meet the needs of our bodies, souls, and spirits. However, only in the place of prayer can we express our dependence on Him to meet these needs.

In Chapter 8, "The Wonders of God's Will," I mentioned Christ's teachings on prayer to His disciples from Matthew 6:9-10. This was to show an example of the role of prayer in creating an avenue for God's will to be reproduced in us. Now I want to refocus on Matthew 6:11-13. In this passage, the Holy Spirit opened my spiritual eyes to see and understand how, through prayer, God desires to supply our daily needs in life's three major areas: *"Give us this day our daily **bread**. And **forgive** us our debts, as we forgive our debtors. And do not lead us into **temptation**, but deliver us from the evil one..."* (Matt. 6:11-13 NKJV).

Each word I emphasized relates to humanity's three basic needs.

Trusting God for Provision

*Give us this day our daily **bread**...* (Matthew 6:11 NKJV).

In this Scripture, Jesus instructed His followers to look to God for daily provision. This prompts the question: What does bread represent? First, it represents food. The provision of food is for the nourishment of the body, which needs daily intake for growth and sustenance. Yet, when facing temptation from satan in the wilderness, Christ declared, *"It is written, 'Man shall not live by bread alone, but by every word that proceeds from the mouth of God'"* (Matt. 4:4 NKJV).

When speaking to the devil, Jesus was in essence saying, "Although I'm hungry and I know I need bread to satisfy My body, listen satan! People are not designed to live by bread alone." Note that He didn't say "not live by bread," but "not live by bread *alone*."

Life requires a combination of physical food and God's written Word, which is spiritual food. *"Every word that proceeds from the mouth of God"* can mean His revealed Word or what God is saying to your spirit at a particular time.

Through prayer, every child of God has a God-given prerogative to depend solely on Him to supply these provisions. Your body is the vessel that houses your soul and spirit. It requires bread to stay alive. God is quite capable of supplying this food, just as He sustained the children of Israel with manna for 40 years in the wilderness (see Deut. 8:2-4). As God's chosen people, they surrendered themselves through Moses' leadership. There is no biblical record of any Israelite dying because of lack of food.

However, what God does one time He won't necessarily do another. I am sure there are people reading this who want to ask, "Since God has the ability to supply our daily bread, is there any need to have a job?" The answer is yes; working to support your physical needs is necessary. Still, it must not represent your ultimate source of security. Too many Christians place their trust in jobs or employers to meet their basic needs. Yet when millions of jobs and "wealth" vanished in the recession beginning in 2007, it served as a reminder that we can never place our trust in humanity or the economy.

This doesn't mean that God is against work. He created work from the beginning of the creation of the world: *"And on the seventh day God ended His work which He had done, and He rested on the seventh day from all His work which He had done"* (Gen. 2:2 NKJV). Other Scriptures support the idea of work as God's plan for the support of our physical needs:

> *You may work and get everything done during six days each week, but the seventh day is a day of rest to honor the Lord your God...* (Deuteronomy 5:13-14).

> *When we were with you, we gave you this rule: "Anyone who refuses to work should not eat." We hear that some people in your group refuse to work. They do nothing but busy themselves in other people's lives. We command those people and beg them in the Lord Jesus Christ to work quietly and earn their own food* (2 Thessalonians 3:10-12).

I believe that what God opposes is trusting in work as our source of supply instead of Him. This kind of attitude puts a job in the place of God. Your work, which is controlled by the world system, is unstable. It is not wise for a child of God to rely on this uncertain means. God's plan is for you to make Him the ultimate Lord of your life, not your job, a person, or anything else. You can have a "secure" job today and watch it vanish tomorrow. If you live in surrender, when your natural means—like the brook that sustained Elijah—dry up, God will provide something better.

> *After a while the stream dried up because there was no rain. Then the Lord spoke His word to Elijah, "Go to Zarephath in Sidon and live there. I have commanded a widow there to take care of you"* (1 Kings 17:7-9).

Living in America for almost five years as a foreign missionary, I had dreams of one day owning a house. From the very first day I came to America, I faithfully began sowing financial seeds and I prayed for God to make this dream a reality. One day in 2005, God spoke to me and said, "It is time for you to buy your house." I said, "But God, you know I have no job and no credit!" God said to me, "You have been faithful, and

I will provide it for you if you will step out in faith." So I went and searched for the kind of house I needed and I found it. I only had a small down payment but with God's intervention my loan was miraculously approved! I have lived in the house for almost five years and I have never missed a mortgage payment and even paid extra toward the principal. God has kept his promise by keeping the heavens open for financial supply just like the story of Zarephath.

A lack of dependence on God encumbers His ability to fulfill His purposes and plans. There are many things God would like to do for His earthly children, but His hands are bound because they have not surrendered to Him. In the Sermon on the Mount, Jesus told the people, *"Seek first God's kingdom and what God wants. Then all your other needs will be met as well"* (Matt. 6:33). On your list of priorities, this is what God expects of you first. He did not ask us to seek after His Kingdom and other things at the same time.

You must decide to become a helpless dependent of God's Kingdom. When you do, other things will be added to your life. The greatest need of the Church today is to surrender to God's divine principles. There is nothing He will withhold from such followers of Christ. *Prayer is the crying expression of our dependence on God's plans and purposes for our lives.*

Forgiveness Is Essential

*And **forgive** us our debts, as we forgive our debtors* (Matthew 6:12 NKJV).

This second key word from Christ's teaching on prayer covers another major human need. Forgiveness of your mistakes, as you forgive those who have offended you, has a direct impact on your soul. The soul is made up of the mind, will, and emotions. If you allow unforgiveness to permeate it, it will affect your thoughts, reasoning, will, decisions, and feelings.

Unforgiveness is a sin that destroys life. As someone once described it, an unforgiving spirit is like an insidious cancer that eats away at a person until it has a deadly impact. Just as physical cancer often can't be seen or felt until it poses serious danger, the cancer of unforgiveness can negatively affect a person's emotions for years. It often can't be readily detected, except through prayer. As you can see through the story that opened this chapter, about my brother's wife being unable to give birth, unforgiveness can steal one's joy, peace, and even health. And it can hinder prayer. This is why Jesus counseled,

> *When you are praying, if you are angry with someone, forgive him so that your Father in heaven will also forgive your sins. But if you don't forgive other people, then your Father in heaven will not forgive your sins* (Mark 11:25-26).

Practicing daily forgiveness is of utmost importance. The writer of Hebrews advised,

> *Pursue peace with all people, and holiness, without which no one will see the Lord: looking carefully lest anyone fall short of the grace of God; lest any root of bitterness springing up cause trouble, and by this many become defiled* (Hebrews 12:14-15 NKJV).

A seed does not immediately become a mature plant; first its roots must be nurtured. The same is true spiritually. Every offense represents a seed that you can allow to sprout in the soil of your soul. If you do, when it is full grown it will reap a bitter harvest. Or you can forgive and cut it off at the roots.

If you don't deal promptly with hurts committed against you, there is a possibility that what sprouts as a tiny seed of bitterness will sink roots deep within your spirit. To keep your soul from such defilement, you need to cry out to God each day to cleanse your heart of bitterness. The praying warrior David kept his soul near to God with such prayers as,

> *Who can understand his errors? Cleanse me from secret faults. Keep back Your servant also from presumptuous sins; let them not have dominion over me. Then I shall be blameless, and I shall be innocent of great transgression. Let the words of my mouth and the meditation of my heart be acceptable in Your sight, O Lord, my strength and my Redeemer* (Psalm 19:12-14 NKJV).

No evil seed can grow in the soil of a soul who surrenders to God in prayer. The person who remains in the prayer closet will constantly receive forgiveness and God's ability to forgive those who sin against him or her.

Turning Back Temptation

> *And lead us not into **temptation**, but deliver us from evil* (Matthew 6:13 NKJV).

Temptation is the gateway to sin, a dangerous poison that kills the life of God in your spirit. The process of spiritual death begins with temptation, followed by lust. After lust comes sin and finally death, which Romans 6:23 says is the wages of sin. This deadly poison has one major goal, to destroy the life of God within your spirit. Yet God has already made provision to keep you from the temptation that leads to sin, which separates your spirit from God.

Sin is a serious matter. Left unconfessed, it will separate you from God. The prophet Isaiah warned, *"It is your evil that has separated you from your God. Your sins cause Him to turn away from you, so He does not hear you"* (Isa. 59:2). Temptation, which many people like to blame on external forces, is also a serious matter. Few will acknowledge that it often stems from their own desires. James wrote,

> *When people are tempted, they should not say, "God is tempting me." Evil cannot tempt God, and God Himself does not tempt anyone. But people are tempted when their own evil desire leads them away and traps them. This desire leads to sin, and then the sin grows and brings death* (James 1:13-15).

God's provision for divine guidance in the face of temptation is only accessible as we learn to express dependence on Him. Only through the weapon of prayer can our spirits remain sensitive to the Spirit's leading. This avoidance is made possible by surrendering daily in prayer. The person who possesses the spirit of prayer overcomes temptation. Jesus made it clear that this is the only way in His encounter with His disciples just before the crucifixion: *"Jesus said to them, 'Why are you sleeping? Get up and pray for strength against temptation"* (Luke 22:46).

Temptation does not give you notice before it strikes, which is why you need to soak your spirit in daily prayer. The first Adam lost fellowship with God through temptation (see Gen. 3:1-13). The last Adam, Jesus Christ, could not be conquered by temptation because He possessed a praying spirit (see Luke 4:1-13). Jesus ultimately overcame every temptation the devil presented, showing that everyone can be tempted, but not everyone can be defeated.

Many believers constantly try to resist satan's temptations, but fail because they don't submit to God. The overpowering force of the devil's tempting can only be conquered as you live in dependence on God. You get to decide how close you want to be with Him. It is your ability to surrender everything through prayer that determines this state. Prayer and a pure heart go hand in hand. Purity of heart follows prayer. The pure in heart will see God, which Jesus promised in the Sermon on the Mount (see Matt. 5:8).

The devil's leading concern is to keep Christians from depending on God through prayer. He trembles at the prayers of a man or woman who submits to God. Take James' advice in this matter:

> *So give yourselves completely to God. Stand against the devil, and the devil will run from you. Come near to God, and God will come near to you. You sinners, clean sin out of your lives. You who are trying to follow God and the world at the same time, make your thinking pure* (James 4:7-8).

The Purpose of Prayer

The prayer of Jesus in the garden of Gethsemane is an example of absolute submission to God.

> *Then Jesus went about a stone's throw away from them. He kneeled down and prayed, "Father, if You are willing, take away this cup of suffering. But do what You want, not what I want"* (Luke 22:41-42).

After a considerable time of meditating on this prayer and pondering its implications, I came to this important conclusion: *The ultimate purpose of prayer is not to see God answer our prayers, but to bring our will into total submission to the will of God.*

When you and I arrive at this point, we will know that prayer blesses all things, brings all things, relieves all things, and prevents all things. Prayer sweetens the bitterness of life, heals the sick, and empowers the feeble. Doubts and fears shrink back in the face of prayer. When you and I touch its purposes, we will see that in prayer all things are truly possible. All those who arrive at the point of complete surrender to God will conclude the wonders of prayer are indeed a reality. I pray that the Holy Spirit will bring you to this point of realization so that your life becomes a wonder to your world.

Pray this prayer:

Father God, today I come to You with all my heart. I have seen how my lack of surrender to Your will and purpose for my life has given the enemy an advantage over me. I receive grace from You, Lord, to bring my will into total submission to Yours. Holy Spirit, empower my prayer life from this day forward and make it a force that causes the devil to tremble. In Jesus' name, amen.

Conclusion

Almost every chapter in this book opened with a true story of the fruits of answered prayer, demonstrating authentic proof of God's reality. Our Lord answers the prayers of His people, obeying the laws that He set forth in His Word. While these stories are exciting, I didn't share them for their dramatic value. I hope that I have provoked you to put prayer to work in your own life that you might see God move in mighty ways, provide for your needs, and defeat your enemies. Trust in the promise of Psalm 56:9: *"On the day I call* [in other words, pray] *for help, my enemies will be defeated. I know that God is on my side."*

Just as natural laws work for any person who puts them into action, so prayer works for anyone who believes in the God who urges us to pray continually. Praying without ceasing is the surest way to maintain a link between Heaven and earth. It is the gateway to the unending flow of Heaven's resources to Christ's followers. Any attempt to live for God on this earth without a proper understanding of the power and blessings that prayer delivers will lead to total frustration. We cannot put our trust in things we can see or in human reasoning; as Second Corinthians 5:7 says, *"For we walk by faith, not by sight"* (KJV). Prayer lines us up with the Source of our faith.

The Bible makes it clear that Heaven governed Jesus' life on earth, leading Him to perform miracles and accomplish His Father's perfect will (see John 5:17,19-20). And it was all because He prayed without ceasing, maintaining a constant connection with His Father. For Christ, prayer meant communing with Him, listening to Him, and watching Him. What was the Father saying? What was the Father doing? What did He desire? The revelations Jesus received, joining His heart and mind to His Father, in turn produced astonishing results throughout His time on earth.

In the same way that the Lord used prayer as the instrument to fulfill His heavenly mission on Earth, He recommends this wonderful tool to us. With it, we will be empowered to complete His will on earth. God's ultimate purpose for our lives is to bring glory to Him; only through prayer and evidence of answered prayer can we effectively complete this task. Scripture constantly tells us to pray because God will answer His people. As Luke 18:1 says, *"Then Jesus used this story to teach His followers that they should always pray and never lose hope."* In John 14:13, He told His disciples, *"And if you ask for anything in My name, I will do it for you so that the Father's glory will be shown through the Son."*

The faithful prayer lives of the first-century believers brought tangible evidence of the power of prayer, which glorified Christ. The miracle at the beautiful gate that Peter and John performed (see Acts 3) is just one of many notable proofs that prayer works. And it can work for everyone who believers in Jesus. However, fearful, overly cautious, hesitant, tentative, half-persuaded, or half-hearted prayers will never produce the power and blessings that prayers of faith will.

It is not enough to have intellectual information about prayer. You must ask the Holy Spirit to give you a revelation of this wonderful privilege and how it can work for you as a believer. Try it now, making today the first day of ongoing daily communication with the heavenly Father. You have nothing to lose and everything to gain. Prayer works.

To contact the author

Global Impact Fellowship Team (Gift)

PO Box 1240

Randallstown, Md 21133 USA

410-588-7820

Email: prayerworks@eguridu.com

IN THE RIGHT HANDS THIS BOOK WILL CHANGE LIVES!

Most of the people that need this message will not be looking for this book. To change their life you need to put a copy of this book in their hands.

> *But others (seeds) fell into good ground, and brought forth fruit, some a hundred-fold, some sixty-fold, some thirty-fold* (Matt. 13:3-8).

Our ministry is constantly seeking methods to find the good ground, the people that need this anointed message to change their life. Will you help us reach these people?

> *Remember this—a farmer who plants only a few seeds will get a small crop. But the one who plants generously will get a generous crop* (2 Cor. 9:6).

EXTEND THIS MINISTRY BY SOWING
3-BOOKS, 5-BOOKS, 10-BOOKS, **OR MORE TODAY,**
AND BECOME A LIFE CHANGER!

Thank you,

Don Nori Sr., Publisher
Destiny Image
Since 1982